£3.00
C8/D

(21)
JMW

Gift Aid item

20 **11343123** 3827

Footprint Hand

Granada &
Sierra Nevada

ANDY SYMINGTON

This is
Granada

The city that became the last outpost of Moorish Spain rules over a spectacular and mountainous province encompassing remote uplands as well as the snowy Sierra Nevada and the dry but fertile valleys of the Alpujarra.

What draws visitors beyond all else, however, is a single monument: the Alhambra. This palace and fortress complex above Granada city is simply magnificent. But Granada is no one-hit wonder; you could happily spend weeks pursuing the spirit of Federico García Lorca, one of Spain's greatest poets, pacing the quiet streets of the Moorish Albayzín district, investigating the Renaissance buildings erected after the Christian conquest and enjoying the classy free tapas in the city's bars.

Overlooking the city is the lofty Sierra Nevada, a protected zone offering year-round outdoor activities. Mulhacén, the peninsula's highest peak, can be climbed in summer, and in winter there's decent skiing. On the south side, the range drops into the valleys of the Alpujarra, where there's great hiking between charmingly compact villages.

Further south, the province has a short coastline known as the Costa Tropical. Although getting more developed, the beachy towns of Almuñécar and Salobreña make tempting stops.

The towns to the east of Granada still have inhabitants who live in caves dug into the rocky hillsides. One of these, Guadix, boasts a fine cathedral; nearby is one of Andalucía's most memorable castles at La Calahorra. On the other side of the provincial capital, the spa town of Alhama and the craggy olive community of Montefrío are excellent places to experience authentic Andalucían *pueblo* life.

Andy Symington

Best of
Granada

❶ The Alhambra

One of Europe's premier sights, this stunning Moorish palace is memorably set over the town against a stunning backdrop of the Sierra Nevada. There's a lot to see here, but it's the exquisite courtyards and stucco work of the Nasrid palace complex that lingers longest in the memory. Page 10.

❷ Cave dwelling

Living in caves has traditionally been a common solution to coping with Granada's chilly winters and scorching summers, and several towns have whole *barrios* of troglodyte residences. Sacromonte in Granada is the most famous, but Guadix and nearby villages also have extensive quarters. There are several options if you want a cave of your own for a night or two. Pages 21 and 67.

❸ The Albayzín

This Moorish quarter is a romantic maze of alleyways, courtyards and unsuspected plazas. Its lower reaches are atmospheric with Moroccan teahouses and market stalls, while its upper areas have great tapas and restaurant venues and some magnificent viewpoints to the Alhambra opposite. Page 24.

❻ Sierra Nevada

Though 'we went skiing in the morning, and swimming in the afternoon' sounds infuriatingly smug, it's actually easily achieved in Granada province. Spain's highest mainland peak is here, and the ski resort still offers good snow even when the beach towns are beginning to fill. Page 45.

❹ Capilla Real

By Granada's cathedral, a chapel sumptuously decorated in late Gothic style houses the mortal remains of the couple who changed the face of Spain and the world: Fernando and Isabel, the Catholic Monarchs. The tombs are fine marble works, and the adjacent museum has intriguing royal items. Page 26.

❺ Federico García Lorca

One of the 20th century's great poets, Lorca was intimately connected with Granada, his hometown. Read some of Lorca's poems while you are visiting the city, take a tour of the house where he spent his summers, then visit the site where he was murdered and the Fountain of Tears. Page 31.

ALBAYZÍN

3

To **2**

1
La Alhambra

4
Capilla Real

5
To Casa Museo de
Federico García Lorca

Baeza — Úbeda

Jimena

Cazorla

JAÉN

Sierra de Cazorla

Parque Natural
Sierra de Castr

Embalse de
Negratín

Freila — Zújar

9
Gorafe — Ba

Baul

Guadahortuna

Torre-
Cárdela

Rute

Montefrío

Illora

Iznalloz

Purullena — Guadix

2

GRANADA

Loja

Río Frío

Moraleda de
Zafayona — Santa Fé

Malá

Cacín

Alhama de
Granada

Ventas de
Huelma

Granada

La Calahorra

8

Puerto del
Suspiro del Moro

Sierra Nevada

6
Pradollano

Sierra de Tejeda

Embalse de
los Bermejales

Padul

Albuñuelas

Béznar

Capileira

7

Trevélez

Yegen — Válor

La Alpujarra

Cádiar

MÁLAGA

Lanjarón

Orgiva

Ferreirola

Otívar

Albondón

Nerja

Salobreña

Motril

Albuñol

Almuñécar

Torrenueva

Los Yesos

La Rábita

10

Carchuna

Costa Tropical

Almerimar

Mediterranean Sea

N

10 km

10 miles

➐ La Alpujarra

South from Granada, these valleys preserved their Moorish culture for long after the Reconquest. Today, their utterly gorgeous white villages make wonderful bases for walking, and have rustic, secluded, accommodation options and earthy local restaurants serving typically hearty traditional cuisine. Page 49.

➑ La Calahorra

This little village is overshadowed by a dramatic and unusual castle that looks rather grim and foreboding from the exterior but has an elaborate Renaissance interior. From here you can hike over a spectacular pass to the Alpujarran valleys. Page 69.

➒ Gorafe

This little-known village is well off the tourist beat but offers a picturesque canyon and an amazing series of Neolithic tombs to explore. Ask at the modern visitor centre for some good background information, then grab a map and plot a path around the prehistoric necropolis. Page 70.

➓ La Costa Tropical

Granada's short coastline has great appeal, with the laid-back, likeable towns of Almuñécar and Salobreña providing a good mix of decent beaches and coves, waterside relaxation, decent eating options and characterful old quarters. Page 73.

Granada city

Most of the popular Western images of Moorish culture – courtyards with delicate fountains, archways sensuously sculpted with arabesques, secluded galleries once paced by viziers and concubines – owe much to the Alhambra, which stands above the city of Granada like a fairyland that might only be accessed by stepping through a wardrobe or by the caprice of a djinn.

It's a place that imposes itself on the visitor's psyche; as well as time spent within its walls, the wanderer in Granada's streets is constantly confronted with a new and unexpectedly sublime view of the fortress and palace, backed (if the weather favours you) by the ridges of the Sierra Nevada. The Alhambra imbues Granada with a tangible romance that this traditionally reactionary city would otherwise struggle to attain.

But while *granadinos* are complaining about the new North African 'invasion', visitors pace the hilltop streets of the Albayzín, discovering atmospheric remnants of Muslim hegemony and Christian conquest. Further into the city, which is studded with bars that lay on free tapas, is some breathtaking Renaissance and Baroque architecture, the tombs of the Catholic Monarchs, as well as the spirit of Federico García Lorca, a giant of 20th-century literature and victim of the thuggery perpetrated away from the frontline of the Spanish Civil War.

a magical closed world of Moorish palaces

★*www.alhambradegranada.org, daily 0830-2000 (1800 Nov-Feb; closed Christmas Day and New Year's Day). Ticket office open 0800-1900 (1700 Nov-Feb). You'll be assigned either a morning ticket (up until 1400) or an afternoon ticket, and an additional half-hour period during which you must enter the Nasrid Palace complex (although you can stay there as long as you choose). It's best to buy your ticket in advance at www.alhambra-tickets.es, or at the La Caixa bank – visit any Spanish branch (Mon-Fri 0830-1400) or T902-888001 from within Spain or T+34-934-923750 from abroad. Choose the day and time you wish to visit, and then pick up your tickets from any La Caixa cash machine (full-price tickets and kids' tickets only), from the machines at the Alhambra ticket office or from the ticket office itself, though expect to queue. If you just turn up at the ticket office, there are long queues, which you can bypass by buying entry at the machines (€1 extra). Expect long waits until your entry slot or a 'come back tomorrow' in busy periods. Tickets cost €14, with a surcharge of €1.40 for prebooking. Seniors and students €9, 12-15 year-olds and disabled visitors €8, under-12s free. If you want to visit the public areas of the Alhambra as well as the extensive gardens around the Generalife, this costs €7.*

Night visits, Mar-Oct Tue-Sat 2200-2330 (ticket office open 2130-2230), Nov-Feb Fri-Sat 2000-2130 (tickets 1930-2030) can be booked in the same way as other tickets and cost the same, or €8 for just the Nasrid Palace complex. If the moon is up and shining into the courtyards, this is an unforgettable experience.

There's not a lot of information posted about the place, so you may want to consider the audio guide for €3 (though it seems to clash with full appreciation of the palace). The official guidebook is €6 in a variety of languages at the ticket office shop. In the ticket office is also a tourist information kiosk. For the disabled, there is an established route that avoids stairs and takes in as much as possible; the ticket office will supply a map and advice.

The approach
Bus and car It's a fabulous experience to walk up to the palace, but a day at the Alhambra is hard on the feet, so you may well want to ascend on wheels. By far the

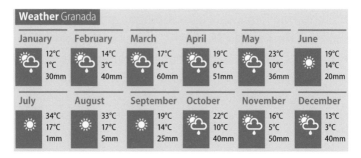

Weather Granada

January	February	March	April	May	June
12°C	14°C	17°C	19°C	23°C	19°C
1°C	3°C	4°C	6°C	10°C	14°C
30mm	40mm	60mm	51mm	36mm	20mm

July	August	September	October	November	December
34°C	33°C	19°C	22°C	16°C	13°C
17°C	17°C	14°C	10°C	5°C	3°C
1mm	5mm	25mm	40mm	50mm	40mm

easiest way to do this is to catch the C3 bus from Plaza Isabel la Católica, which zips up the hill every five minutes or so. If you're thinking of driving, it's likely to take you longer to get to the Alhambra than on foot, but there are two ways; a serpentine route that ascends from off Calle Molinos, or a purpose-built back road that leaves the Ronda Sur bypass, which in turn comes off the *circunvalación* which circles the north and west of the city. It's well signposted; if arriving from outside town, don't leave the bypass until you see the Alhambra signs. Depending on how busy the car parks are, you may have to park a fair walk away from the entrance.

On foot If you are walking up, it's a steepish climb. Most visitors ascend via the Cuesta de Gomérez from the Plaza Nueva; here a different ascent is suggested, and the Cuesta can be used for the return trip.

At one end of Plaza Nueva is the Church of Santa Ana. Keeping it on your right, follow the course of the river along a cobbled street (this walk is detailed on page 21). The Alhambra will soon become visible above you to your right. Reaching the end of the café-lined promenade known as Paseo de los Tristes, turn right and cross the bridge. From here a pretty path called Cuesta del Rey Chico (also known as Cuesta de los Chinos) ascends gently directly to the Alhambra. It's a fine little walk: after passing under the mighty bridge leading to the Generalife, you emerge alongside a restaurant; turn left and you'll be at the ticket office.

If you've pre-purchased your ticket and your entry slot for the Nasrid Palace is a long way off, it's a good idea to head for the Generalife (see page 20) first, before

(this walk is detailed on page 21)

the Generalife (see page 20)

Essential Granada

Getting around

Walking is the best option for getting about, but Granada is a hilly place so you may want to use public transport. Tired feet will love buses C3 and C4, which ascend from Plaza Isabel la Católica to the Alhambra. Bus C1 does a circuit from Calle Reyes Católicos around the Albayzín, while C2 heads into Sacromonte. The LAC line runs long buses on a high-density loop around the centre of town; all other buses are routed to connect with it at some point, so cross-city journeys typically involve catching the LAC then transferring (free) to another bus, or vice versa. A ticket on a local bus costs €1.20. An online journey planner in Spanish is at www.transportesrober. com. Taxis are also readily available and cheap.

Best places to stay

Carmen de la Alcubilla del Caracol, page 34
Cuevas El Abanico, page 34
Casa Morisca, page 34
Hotel Santa Isabel la Real, page 35
Hotel Párragasiete, page 36

When to go

Like most of inland Andalucía, Granada gets powerfully hot in summer. Winters are cold; general visit to the city, spring and autumn are the best periods.

Best tapas bars

Casa Enrique, page 39
La Brujidera, page 39
Bodegas Espadafor, page 40

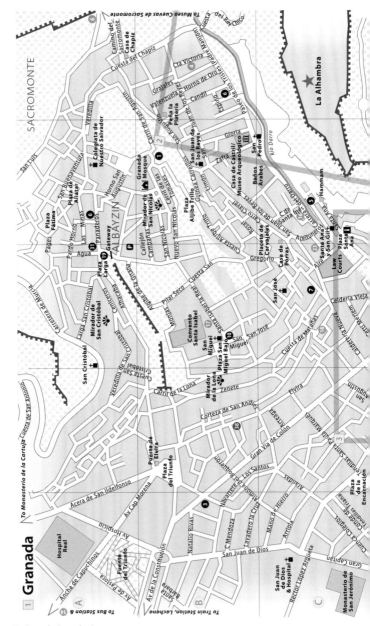

Granada

SACROMONTE

To Monasterio de la Cartuja

To Monasterio de la Cartuja · Cuesta de San Antonio

To Museo Cuevas de Sacromonte

La Alhambra

Hospital Real

Fuente del Triunfo

Plaza del Triunfo

Plaza Fátima

Plaza de Buenaventura

Plaza de Aliatar

ALBAYZIN

Mirador de San Cristóbal

San Cristóbal

Colegiata de Nuestro Salvador

Casa de Chapiz

Camino del Sacromonte

Cuesta del Chapiz

Granada Mosque

Mirador de San Nicolás

Plaza Aljibe Trillo

Casa de Castril/ Museo Arqueológico

Baños Árabes

San Pedro

Río Darro

Hammam

Convento Santa Isabel

San Miguel

Plaza San Miguel Bajo

Mirador de la Lona

Puerta de Elvira

Law Courts

Santa Ana Plaza

Placeta de Carvajales

Casa de Porras

San José

Plaza de la Encarnación

Monasterio de San Jerónimo

San Juan de Dios & Hospital

To Bus Station &

To Train Station, Lachana

Gran Vía de Colón

Acera de San Ildefonso

Gran Capitán

12·Granada Granada city

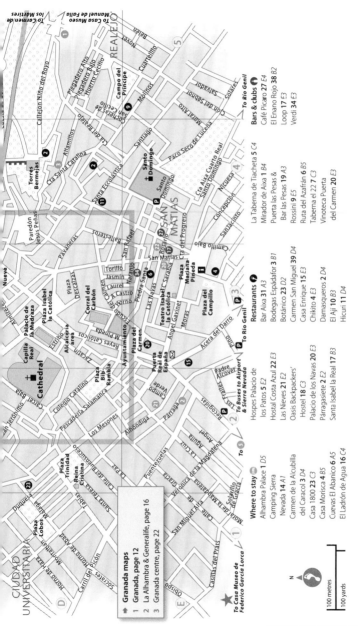

Granada maps

1 Granada, page 12
2 La Alhambra & Generalife, page 16
3 Granada centre, page 22

Where to stay

Alhambra Palace 1 D5
Camping Sierra Nevada 14 A1
Carmen de la Alcubilla del Caracol 3 D4
Casa 1800 23 C3
Casa Morisca 4 B5
Cuevas El Abanico 6 A5
El Ladrón de Agua 16 C4
Hospes Palacio de los Patos 5 E2
Hostal Costa Azul 22 E3
Las Nieves 21 E2
Oasis Backpackers' Hostel 18 B3
Palacio de los Navas 20 E3
Parragasiete 2 E2
Santa Isabel la Real 17 B3

Restaurants

Bar Aixa 31 A3
Bodegas Espadafor 3 B1
Botánico 23 D2
Carmen San Miguel 39 D4
Casa Enrique 15 E3
Chikito 4 E3
Damasqueros 2 D4
El Ají 10 B3
Hicuri 11 D4
La Taberna de Tiacheta 5 C4
Mirador de Aixa 1 B4
Puerta las Pesas & Bar las Pesas 19 A3
Rossini 9 B5
Ruta del Azafrán 6 B5
Taberna el 22 7 C3
Vinoteca Puerta del Carmen 20 E3

Bars & clubs

Café Pícaro 27 E4
El Enano Rojo 38 B2
Loop 17 E3
Verdi 34 E3

returning to the main centre of the Alhambra. If it is fairly soon, head directly towards the Alcazaba and the principal buildings. That route is followed here.

Follow the signs for the Alcazaba and Palacios Nazaríes. Passing through the checkpoint, you descend the main street of the Alhambra complex, the Calle Real. This used to be the heart of the Moorish town within the Alhambra, and the location of the main mosque and the Baños del Polinario, or public baths. The baths are still in good shape; go in and admire their brickwork and horseshoe arches. There's some stucco work preserved, but best are the typical star-shaped holes in the ceiling. In this building, which was also once a tavern, is a small museum dedicated to the Granadan composer Angel Barrios. Next door, where the mosque once stood, is the early 17th-century church of Santa María, even more out of place here than the Palace of Carlos V, which is the next building.

Palacio de Carlos V

Many words have been written in prosecution and defence of this building, unmistakeable with its massive modern-looking blocks of stone studded with huge rings held in the mouths of lions and eagles. As a Renaissance building in its own right, it has several striking features. The core of most complaints is its heavy-handedness in comparison with the delicate dignity of the Muslim palace, part of which was demolished to accommodate it. But it's easy to be tough on Carlos; he liked the Nasrid Palace well enough to use it as his own quarters, and if he had simply built his palace over the Nasrid one, as was the custom of both Moors and Christians in those days, the issue would never have arisen.

The palace was never finished in Carlos's lifetime – indeed the roof went on only in the 20th century. Construction had been funded by taxes raised from the Moriscos – the nominally converted descendants of the Moors – but with their major rebellion in 1568, it ground to a halt. What remains is impressive, but definitely grandiose rather than subtle. The southern portal is supported on Ionic columns and has figures of Victory, Fame and Fertility over the door, as well as panels with mythological scenes and the arms of Carlos V. This contrasts with the western Doric entrance, with escutcheons carved with Hercules and Atlas flanking the arms of Felipe II; below are scenes of the battle of Pavia.

Most of the building is taken up by the circular central courtyard, an imposing space with superb acoustics; try whispering from the centre. While the octagonal chapel features temporary exhibitions, most of the rooms of the palace are taken up by the **Museo de la Alhambra** ① *Wed-Sat 0830-1800 or 2000, Tue and Sun 0830-1400 or 1430, free with Alhambra ticket*, and **de Bellas Artes** ① *Tue-Sat 1000-1700 summer, 1000-1800 winter, 1000-2030 spring and autumn, Sun 1000-1700; EU citizens free, others €1.50*. The former, on the ground floor, describes itself as having 'the world's best collection of Nasrid art'; not such an impressive claim considering that the Nasrids were purely a Granadan dynasty. The museum, though, is well worth a visit. There are many tiled and stuccoed panels from the site itself, as well as the fine painted Jar of the Gazelles, a 15th-century urn 1.5 m high. The Fine Arts museum upstairs has a collection of works from Granadine artists and some fine religious pieces, especially sculptures by Diego de Siloé, Alonso Cano and Pedro de Mena. An enamel triptych

BACKGROUND
Alhambra

Of all Spain's tens of thousands of historical monuments, the Alhambra stands supreme. The final manifestation of the doomed Moorish civilization in the peninsula, its history also mirrors that of Spain in the succeeding six centuries. Taken by Fernando and Isabel in a surge that culminated in Catholic Spain ruling vast tracts of Europe and the New World, it, like the country, eventually fell into dereliction and then use as a barracks in the war-torn 19th century. Rediscovered by Romantic travellers, it is now one of Europe's most-visited destinations, with over two million visitors annually.

The defensible hills were the principal reason why the Zirid rulers moved their town from nearby Elvira to Granada in the early 11th century. A natural fortress, the Sabika hill on which the Alhambra stands had previously been used by the Romans and Visigoths, but only a few remnants have been found from those eras. The Zirids fortified the hill, although their main palace was on the facing Albayzín. The Alhambra as we see it today was principally a construction of the later Nasrid dynasty, who rose to power in the 1230s and established the hill as their seat of power. The Nasrids ruled Granada until 1492 and are responsible for most of the many buildings that form the Alhambra complex. Of these, their royal palace complex is what inspires visitors with the most awe. After Boabdil surrendered the city and fortress to the Catholic Monarchs, many modifications were made to the existing structures, and several new edifices were thrown up, not least of which is the bulky Renaissance Palacio de Carlos V. The name Alhambra is from the Arabic *al-qalat al-hamra*, meaning the red fort, perhaps from the colour of the sandstone, especially in the setting sun.

from Limoges features El Gran Capitán, but the museum is unfortunately placed; it's hard to resist the call of the Alhambra's many other attractions. There's also a reasonable book and souvenir shop on the ground floor of the building.

La Alcazaba

From the Palacio de Carlos V, head through the monumental gateway known as the Puerta del Vino – for it was used in Christian times to store wine – to the large open space in front of the Alcazaba. La Alcazaba, the fortress part of the compound, is muscular, unashamedly functional and highly impressive. Older than the rest of the buildings on the site, much of its finer features were destroyed by Napoleon's troops in the Peninsular War. Its effective defensive design is immediately evident upon entering, as you are forced to walk along a narrow passageway overlooked by high towers. Climb the one at the corner, the **Torre del Homenaje** (Tower of Homage), for views, before crossing the large central courtyard. This was once covered with dwellings housing the soldiers who defended the complex. The high **Torre de la Vela** (watchtower) looms large over the city and has a spectacular panorama. Directly across from you is the hill of the Albayzín with its flood of white houses, while to the left stretches the modern city. Turning further to the left, you can see an earlier fortification on the next hill; these are the **Torres Bermejas** (Vermilion Towers). They're actually more of a light orange in colour if you walk to them; you can't enter, but there's a good restaurant at the base. The large orange castellated affair further along the ridge is the Alhambra Palace hotel. On 2 January, the Torre de la Vela is filled with *granadinos* queuing to have a go at ringing the bell; if a single woman does so, it's said that she'll be engaged within the year. You exit the Alcazaba through a long formal garden. In the centre of it is a fountain that used to stand atop the fountain in the Court of Lions in the Nasrid Palace.

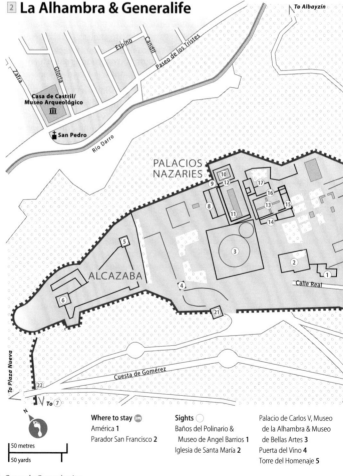

2 La Alhambra & Generalife

To Albayzín

Zafra
Gloria
Espino
Candil
Paseo de los Tristes

Casa de Castril/
Museo Arqueológico

San Pedro

Río Darro

PALACIOS
NAZARIES

ALCAZABA

Calle Real

To Plaza Nueva

Cuesta de Gomérez

N

50 metres
50 yards

To 7

Where to stay
América 1
Parador San Francisco 2

Sights
Baños del Polinario &
Museo de Angel Barrios 1
Iglesia de Santa María 2

Palacio de Carlos V, Museo
de la Alhambra & Museo
de Bellas Artes 3
Puerta del Vino 4
Torre del Homenaje 5

Palacios Nazaríes

No matter what alterations and restructuring have taken place, even though the original bright colours have completely faded away, this ensemble of Moorish palaces is one of staggering architectural and artistic achievement. Many visitors are left in a sort of amazed incomprehension after passing through the elaborate patios and halls.

To move beyond this, it is helpful to have some understanding of Islamic architectural principles. While it is untrue that Islam prohibits the depiction of human or animal figures (although at certain periods prevailing fundamentalism

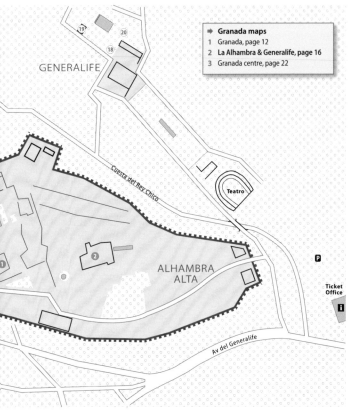

➡ **Granada maps**	
1	Granada, page 12
2	**La Alhambra & Generalife, page 16**
3	Granada centre, page 22

has certainly discouraged it), they are not a common decorative theme; vegetal and geometric motifs form the bulk of the decoration. Perhaps the fundamental principle of the Alhambra is that of levels, or hierarchy. As certain chambers within the building are clearly attributable by size and ornateness to different strata of the royal entourage, so the decoration of each room follows this theme. Small and intricate pieces of pattern join to form a larger design; as our focus widens, the design widens with it. A tiny *mocárab* or tiled motif, perfect in itself, becomes merely a star in an entire firmament. This has clear theological overtones, and the message is reinforced by the Arabic phrases repeated over and over around rooms and by visionary poems that clearly describe the Alhambra as a small jewel reflecting the unimaginable grandeur of Allah.

The palaces are entered through the **Mexuar**, still a fine space although much meddled with by both the Nasrid rulers and then the Catholic Monarchs, who converted what was once a reception hall into a chapel. Despite this, you'll notice several features that recur throughout the building. The ceramic dado decorated with coloured polygons is typical, as is the inlaid wooden ceiling (restored) and the arches with their *mocárabes* (concave depressions forming an array of icicle-like points). The capitals of the columns are particularly fine and preserve much original colour. The gallery was put in when the conversion to chapel took place. Beyond the hall is an angled prayer-room with a *mihrab* accurately aligned towards Mecca and windows looking over the Albayzín.

You'll soon arrive at a small courtyard with a fountain, known as the **Patio del Cuarto Dorado**. The northern arcade has impressive stucco and arabesques, while the room off here has a gilt wooden ceiling put in by the Catholic Monarchs. However, the space is dominated by the high façade of the **Salón de Comares**, constructed around 1370. Under its elegant wooden eaves is amazingly intricate decoration, all of which was brightly coloured until as recently as the mid-19th century. Going through this façade, we are faced not with an equally monumental hallway, but with a cramped space with small corridors leading off it. The Nasrids knew that, amid all this earthly delight, their days were numbered, and defence remained an important consideration.

Twisting through to your left, you emerge in the **Patio de los Arrayanes** (Court of the Myrtles), centred on a large pool of water that seems to have been designed to exactly fit the reflections of the two large façades at either end of it. Both of these rest on a portico of seven round arches topped with perforated plasterwork known as *sebka*. The porticos end in alcoves richly adorned with *mocárabes*, which preserve some blue colouring. On the near side, you pass through the **Sala de la Barca**, named for the Arabic inscription *baraka*, or blessing, that adorns the wall (and not because the restored 20th-century ceiling resembles a boat, or *barca*, as some tour guides solicitously point out), and into the high **Salón de Comares**, surrounded by highly adorned alcoves. Part of the gilt ceramic floor remains and every inch of the room is intricately decorated. Gaze on the wooden ceiling and its hierarchy of stars, plausibly claimed to represent the seven heavens and the eighth, at the centre, wherein resides Allah. Although on first count you'll likely only see six rows of stars, the seventh may become clear before you get dizzy. The ceiling is reconstructed from fragments, but

BACKGROUND
Granada

The site of Granada was originally settled in the first millennium BC, when it was an Iberian hilltop town known as Elybirge. Taken over by the Romans, who named it Illiberis, it grew in importance during the Visigothic period; at this time a Jewish district known as **Garnatha Alheyud** was established on the southern slopes of the Alhambra hill.

After the Moors took control, the town's name became Elvira, based on nearby hills, and the Jewish part **Garnata**; the latter name has persisted. It was under the control of the caliphate of Córdoba, and then became the capital of an important *taifa* state. As the Christians advanced into Andalucía, taking cities such as Córdoba and Sevilla, there was a huge influx of Muslim refugees to Granada, where the nobleman Mohammed Ibn-Yusuf Ibn-Nasr had set himself up as ruler here in 1237, giving his name to the Nasrid dynasty. With the Christians in such bullish mood, it was decided to construct a bigger and better fortification on the hill opposite the Albayzín; its reddish hue led to its name, **Al-Qalat Al-Hamra**, or the red fort. Most of what we see in the Alhambra today was built during the reigns of Yusuf I (1334-1354) and Mohammed V (1354-1391), at which time the city was very prosperous. The Granada emirate was effectively a vassal state of the Christian kingdoms surviving by paying tribute. Once Fernando and Isabel set their sights on conquering it, the city was doomed to fall. After dynastic strife and vacillations that rendered the Moors' last days more comedy than a tragedy, the last emir of Granada, Boabdil, surrendered the keys of the city to the Catholic Monarchs on New Year's Day in 1492 after a siege. The immediate expulsion of the nation's Jews hit Granada hard, and once the Moors and Moriscos had followed, the city had lost vital segments of its population.

The city prospered somewhat with the new American trade routes, and a number of Renaissance and Baroque monuments were erected, but Granada was gradually becoming a provincial backwater. The Peninsular War hit the city especially hard, with French troops heavily damaging the Alhambra while using it as a barracks. It was in this decaying atmosphere that Washington Irving and others visited, raising awareness of the Moorish majesty of the city that has made it enduringly popular with visitors ever since. The 19th century also saw a number of questionable urban projects, such as the covering of the river and the bulldozing of the Gran Vía through part of the old town.

In the early part of the 20th century, Granada had a full-scale cultural revival, with the poet Federico García Lorca and the composer Manuel de Falla prominent and active in promoting Andalucían heritage. This came to an abrupt end. Although Granada had been an actively liberal city early in the 19th century, it was steadfastly nationalist by the time the Civil War came along, and the local fascists slaughtered thousands of moderates and left-wingers, including Lorca.

has recaptured the impact of the original. It is thought that this was an important state room where the Nasrid rulers received guests.

At the other end of the Court of Myrtles, the façade is just that, since Charles V knocked down that part of the palace to park his own construction alongside. So after examining the other chambers around the court, head through into the most-photographed part of the ensemble, the **Patio de los Leones**, or Court of Lions. Here the grace of the Moorish design reaches new heights. Framing the central fountain propped up by 12 lovable kings of beasts is a fantasy of stonework. Two pavilions supported by the slenderest of columns and most delicate of arches face each other across the courtyard, the whole of which is framed by an elegant colonnade. Stop and linger, then move anti-clockwise around the courtyard. On the first of the long sides is the **Sala de los Abencerrajes**, graced by a cupola of *mocárabes*. It was here that Boabdil was supposed to have had the leading members of the Abencerraje family murdered one by one; the proof is the 'blood stains' in the fountain.

At the far end of the Court of Lions is the **Sala de los Reyes**, whose alcoves feature a range of paintings on sheepskin, depicting in contrast with the rest of the palace, portraits of seated rulers and a range of knightly scenes. They bear clear Christian influences and some scholars feel that they must have been painted by Italian artists resident in the Nasrid city.

The next chamber, the **Sala de Dos Hermanas** has another grand cupola similar to that of the **Sala de los Abencerrajes** opposite. The adjoining **Sala de los Ajimeces** has perhaps the most romantic of the Alhambra's lookouts, the **Mirador de Lindaraja**, from the original Arabic meaning eyes of Aixa's house (Aixa was the mother of the last Moorish ruler Boabdil). Originally it would have looked over a garden and beyond to the city. The tiny chamber is as perfect as anything here, with its dado of coloured tiles, stucco work and ceiling embedded with stained glass.

Beyond here, the **Imperial chambers** were built as the residence of Carlos V; Washington Irving stayed in a room off here. There are more excellent views over the Albayzín from here; you descend and exit through a pair of patios, off one of which are the original Moorish baths, again with star-shaped skylights for steam to exit.

After exiting, and even though you may well be overwhelmed by stuccoed splendour, keep going ahead and to your left to examine two more small buildings, the **Palacio del Pórtico**, a small, earlier palace fronted by an elegant pool, and next to it, a sublime little oratory with an elaborate *mihrab*.

Generalife

Retracing your steps towards the ticket office, follow the signs for the Generalife. Although it could be an insurance company, the name of this summer palace separated from the bulk of the Alhambra's buildings is usually accepted to mean 'the gardens of the master builder'. It is indeed surrounded by gardens, but these were mostly planted in the 19th and 20th centuries and perhaps bear little resemblance to the original Moorish design. The walk to the Generalife is down a grove of cypress and jasmine; the building is entered through a controversially renovated doorway marked with the symbol of the key of Allah. Passing through a courtyard, you emerge into the **Patio de la Acequia**, an extensive space marked by an array of criss-cross water jets that sprinkle into a long pool. The belvedere, which gives fine views, was a Christian addition, such openness being anathema to the Moors, who preferred to look out only from the small mirador halfway along, decorated with 14th-century stucco. A herb garden along the pool scents the air. At the end of the patio is the **Sala Regia**, or royal hall, accessed via a five-arched portico. The hall is small but well proportioned, with fine *mocárabes* on the capitals and cornice and a small delicate mirador. The repeated inscription reads "There is one and only one conqueror, and that is Allah". The top floor was added by the Catholic Monarchs; from it there are views of the Albayzín and the caves of Sacromonte, but to reach it you first pass through the **Patio de los Cipreses** (Court of the Cypresses). This was once a place to bathe, and the tree is said to have borne witness to the seduction of the luckless Boabdil's wife by a noble of the Abencerraje family, an indiscretion that may have led to the massacre of the clan.

After visiting the top floor, ascend to the upper gardens by way of the water staircase, which has a stream flowing down the banisters, yet another example of Moorish hydrological genius. This garden is full of squirrels, who are keenly watched by the Alhambra's vast population of semi-feral cats.

Leaving the Alhambra

When you're ready to leave the Alhambra, walk back to the courtyard in front of the Alcazaba and turn left to descend through the **Torre de la Justicia** (Gate of Justice), the most impressive of the Alhambra's remaining gateways. Turn as you pass through it and note the Islamic motifs of the key and the hand engraved on the outside. Washington Irving was told that on the day the hand reached down to grasp the key, the Alhambra would crumble to dust and the buried gold of the Moors would be revealed. Below here is an ornate fountain from the time of Carlos V, with three grotesque heads and pomegranate symbols. Descend from here down an avenue lined with elms planted by the Duke of Wellington to the **Puerta de las Granadas**, or Gate of the Pomegranates. From here the Cuesta de Gomérez descends to Plaza Nueva.

Plaza Nueva to Sacromonte
a great walk along the Darro, with spectacular Alhambra views

★The Darro is one of Granada's two rivers, but is usually no more than a mountain stream, although it's a mouse that occasionally roars and floods the Albayzín and Sacromonte. It actually flows through much of central Granada but its course has been gradually paved over. You can see it emerge from its tunnel to merge with the larger Río Genil at Puente Blanco, at the end of Acera del Darro. It enters the tunnel just off Plaza Nueva and you can follow its course upstream from here. (Alternatively, you can take bus C2 from Plaza Nueva all the way into Sacromonte.)

Start off in **Plaza Nueva** with its terraced cafés that you're really better off avoiding. On the north side of the plaza is the large building of the law courts. It has a Renaissance patio designed by Diego de Siloé, but you'll probably only get past security if you look like you have a reason to be there.

At the end of the plaza is the church of **Santa Ana y San Gil**, built on the site of a mosque in the early 16th century. The bell tower that peers over the river features fine *mudéjar* tilework, while the doorway (you can discern the bricked-in entrance of the original mosque) is flanked by stately cypresses. If you can get in (it opens for the 1830 mass at around 1800) you'll be struck by the ornate Baroque side chapels and wooden ceiling. The church is crowded with sculpture and paintings, particularly around the gallery. An arch, no doubt part of the original structure, separates the chancel from the nave.

Follow the Darro, leaving the church on your right. Passing picturesque stone bridges, this is one of Granada's nicest walks, and is well stocked with tapas bars.

In its heyday, Granada would have had dozens of bathhouses in the Albayzín, but the **Baños Arabes** ⓘ *Cra del Darro 31, T958-229738, summer daily 0930-1430, 1700-2100, winter 1000-1700, entry free at time of research but due to be charged,* is the only one that retains more than fragments. Many tourists pass by the understated façade; make sure you visit during your stay. While the baths were used as a communal laundry in the 19th century, they became a private residence. After passing through a patio, you enter the baths, which are extraordinarily well

3 Granada centre

Granada maps
1 Granada, page 12
2 La Alhambra & Generalife, page 16
3 Granada centre, page 22

Where to stay 🛏
Hostal Navarro Ramos 2

Restaurants 🍴
Antigua Bodegas
Castañeda 4

Bar León 5
Bodega La Mancha 13
Heladería Tiggiani 3
La Brujidera 7
Taberna Salinas 10

Bars & clubs 🎵
La Estrella 11

N

50 metres
50 yards

preserved. It's a place of marvellous peace with its star-shaped air vents in the ceiling admitting a delicate light. It was open to men and women on alternate days. The Catholic Monarchs shut down the bathhouses pretty rapidly when they took Granada; they were appalled at the unhealthy idea of washing off the protective coating of filth that coated Christians at the time (Isabel claimed to only have washed twice in her life; that was twice more than many people, one suspects); they also feared (more understandably) that the bathhouses would become centres of sedition and plots.

A little beyond the baths, the river is spanned by the remains of a horseshoe arch that once formed part of the Alhambra's fortifications.

Granada's **Museo Arqueológico** ⓘ *Cra del Darro 43, closed for renovations at time of research but hoped to open in 2015 or 2016*, is housed in the Casa de Castril, a 16th-century mansion with an admirable Plateresque façade that could be a textbook example of the style, with its coats of arms, courtly symbols, shells, beasts and intricate stonework. The collection is strong; many of Andalucía's most interesting prehistoric finds are from caves in this province. There's an ancient fossilized skull of an *elephas meridionalis* mammoth and much material from grave sites, including amazing material from Albuñol, a gold torc and pieces of woven basket that are nearly 6000 years old. Bronze Age pot burials are well displayed, as are a series of alabaster funerary jars originally from Egypt. A bronze astrolabe is the highlight of the Moorish section; dating from 1481, it's a phenomenal piece of craftsmanship and testament to the high-powered scientific tradition of the Muslim world.

The narrow Carrera del Darro widens into the **Paseo de los Tristes**, named because funeral processions used to pass this way en route to the cemetery atop the Alhambra hill. The Alhambra itself looms over it; you can admire it from the terrace of one of the cafés here. Reaching the end of the promenade, you can turn right up the footpath to the Alhambra (see page 10), or left up the hill called the Cuesta del Chapiz. The massive house and gardens on the opposite bank of the river is the **Carmen de los Chapiteles**, once home of El Gran Capitán, the general Gonzalo de Córdoba, and now used for cultural events and conferences.

Ascending the Cuesta, turn right at the Moorish Casa de Chapiz to enter the barrio of **Sacromonte**. Built along a hillside, most of the houses here are caves. Until the 1960s it was home to most of Granada's gypsy population, and a few still live here, though the increasingly fashionable zone is now one of Granada's trendiest and most expensive. There are a number of touristy flamenco shows put on here in the evenings (see Flamenco, page 41). Wandering through the area, you may still be invited into a gypsy cave home, where you'll be treated to a personal flamenco show; you'll be expected to pay heavily.

It's a very picturesque place to stroll in the sun; the homes are all whitewashed; the doors and windows trimmed with blue, and prickly pears stud the hillside. At the top of the district is the **Museo Cuevas del Sacromonte** ⓘ *C Barranco de los Negros s/n, T958-215120, www.sacromontegranada.com, winter 1000-1800, summer 1000-2000, €5*, an ethnographic museum well set out in a series of caves, which is pricey but has some good displays on traditional crafts such as basketwork and weaving. There's also a café and good viewpoint.

★The Albayzín (or Albaicín), which rises above the Darro on the opposite bank to the Alhambra, was once the residence of the bulk of the city's population and is filled with Moorish remnants. More than similar quarters in other Andalucían cities, the Albayzín has retained a distinctly Islamic atmosphere. This is partly due to the narrow street plan and whitewashed houses, partly due to the sublime vistas of the Alhambra that open up at unexpected moments, and partly due to the presence of a significant North African population. Moroccan- and Algerian-run craft shops, teahouses and restaurants line the region's lower reaches, while near the top is a mosque.

The best way to ascend to the Albayzín for the first time is from Calle de Elvira, turning up **Calle Calderería Nueva**, lined with teahouses and Moroccan shops. At a small square, fork left up the hill following Cuesta San Gregorio. After a short distance, turn right at Calle del Beso (Street of the Kiss) and drop into the small Plaza de Porras.

On this plaza is the 16th-century mansion of **Casa de Porras**, now a cultural centre with art exhibitions. Enter and admire the central patio.

Continuing through the square, you'll come to the **Placeta de Carvajales**, reached by a flight of steps up to your left. This offers a peaceful bench or two to enjoy stunning vistas of the Alcazaba part of the Alhambra. Bookmark the spot as one to come back to at night, when the view is even more memorable.

Leaving the plaza without going down the stairs, turn left, which will bring you back to Cuesta San Gregorio; follow it up the hill to the right. Coming to Plaza Aljibe Trillo, you could take a short detour to your right then left. At the bottom of Calle Limón, look out for the dilapidated church of **San Juan de los Reyes**, with a beautiful ex-minaret with blind arches and delicate tracery. Just beyond, on Calle Zafra, there's a 15th-century Moorish house visible down the slope.

Back in Plaza Aljibe Trillo, follow the *cuesta* of the same name up the hill. Taking your third left, you'll emerge in a square by a church. The **Colegiata de Nuestro Salvador** ⓘ *Mon-Sat 1000-1300, 1630-1830, €1*, was built over the main mosque of the Albayzín in the 16th to 18th centuries. Burned down in the lead-up to the Spanish Civil War, the church is mostly reconstructed and of limited interest apart from a secluded Moorish patio filled with lemon trees and horseshoe arches. It's a simple and likeable space; the strict Almohads who built it in the 12th century had little regard for ornamentation. The other Moorish remnant is the bell tower, transformed from a minaret by Diego de Siloé.

Near here, the **Mirador de San Nicolás** is the most popular spot to sit and enjoy the sun setting on the Alhambra opposite. Despite being crowded with locals and tourists, the views are worth watching, as they are at night, when the complex is floodlit.

Adjacent to the mirador is the **Granada mosque** ⓘ *www.mezquitadegranada.com, gardens open 1000-1400, 1800-2130*, with a formal garden open to the public, and a centre of Islamic studies. The *mihrab* is a replica of that in the Mezquita at Córdoba.

ON THE ROAD

The place to be at sunset

Less thronged than the popular Mirador de San Nicolás is one higher up, the Mirador de San Cristóbal, which gives good, if more distant, views of the Alhambra and a spectacular perspective over the city and the mountains that surround it. It's the place to be at sunset.

You can get there by taking a right up Cuesta San Cristóbal as you descend Calle Alhacaba from Plaza Larga. Otherwise follow Cuesta de San Antonio from the Hospital Real (turning right at the crossroads) by following signs for Murcia from the northern part of town, or by catching bus C2 from Gran Vía. Get off at the church of San Cristóbal; the mirador is opposite. The whole of Granada is displayed before you, including the walls of the Albayzínn. Flitting bats are backed by the peaks of the Sierra Nevada. Stunning.

Returning to the Colegiata, follow Calle Panaderos down to the tree-shaded Plaza Larga, a popular locals' hang-out by day but usually deserted at night. There's an impressive Moorish gateway at one end of it. From here head to Plaza San Miguel Bajo. The easy way is through the arch, straight ahead, and take the second right down Camino Nuevo San Nicolás. The hillier route, however, is a better option if you've still got plenty of energy. From Plaza Larga, head straight down the hill, Calle Alhacaba. You'll get a cracking view of the Almohad city walls on your left (the council will one day open a walkway along them, which will be accessed by the gate at the end of Plaza Larga).

The road eventually leads down to the impressive Puerta de Elvira, which was once the main gateway into the city. Before you've descended the whole way, though, turn left up Carril de la Lona past another gateway (unless sunset is approaching, in which case see box, above). Take the left (steeper) fork and at the top of the hill you'll reach the mirador of La Lona. Turn left to find yourself in **Plaza San Miguel Bajo**.

This is one of the most endearing parts of the Albayzín, a lopsided square lined on one side by chestnut trees. The Diego de Siloé façade of the 16th-century San Miguel church looms over the square; the church preserves its cistern from its early days as a mosque. On the plaza opposite is a *crucero*, Cristo de las Lañas (Christ of the Clamps; after being broken to pieces in the Civil War, he was clamped together and repaired by locals who had guarded the pieces). There are several good places to eat here.

Near Plaza San Miguel Bajo is the convent of Santa Isabel, erected by the Catholic Monarchs, whose symbols of the yoke and arrows can be seen on the lavish Isabelline façade of the church. It's still populated by nuns; the church's opening is irregular, but you can try to sneak a peek just before 1830 mass; note the fine *mudéjar* ceiling.

When you're ready to leave the Albayzín, head down Calle San Miguel, which becomes Calle San José and has a 16th-century church of the same name. Its bell tower was inevitably once a minaret, and is constructed of beautifully irregular stone; there's a horseshoe arched window halfway up dating from the 10th century. The church also preserves its *aljibe*, the cistern used for ritual washing before prayer.

Keep heading straight ahead and you'll come once again to Cuesta San Gregorio, where a right turn will lead you back to Calle de Elvira.

The Catedral and around

home of the sepulchres of Spain's most influential monarchs

Catedral

Gran Vía s/n, T958-222959. Apr-Oct Mon-Sat 1045-1945, Sun 1600-1845, Nov-Mar Mon-Sat 1045-1315, 1600-1845, Sun 1600-1845. €4; audio guide €3.

After the Reconquest, Granada's main mosque was consecrated as a cathedral and used for three decades until it was levelled and a new cathedral begun in 1521. The project changed architectural course several times and wasn't really finished; by the time it was ready for its final touches a couple of centuries later, interest and cash had long since dwindled.

The cathedral leaves many visitors cold, but it needn't. It was largely designed by the great early Renaissance master Diego de Siloé, and much of the artworks are by the hand of the versatile Alonso Cano, a temperamental 17th-century all-rounder equally adept with brush, chisel or graph paper in hand. One unlikely story claims that he was forced to seek asylum in the cathedral after being accused of murdering his wife. The bishop let him stay, but only on condition that he set about decorating the place.

Before entering the building, stroll around to its southwestern façade, best viewed from a couple of blocks down the street. Executed by Cano, its triple arch exudes purity of form and simplicity. Along the northwestern side of the building are some intriguing open-air spice stalls exuding rich aromas.

Inside, you will be immediately struck by the lightness of the white interior, giving it a most un-Spanish feel. In fact, because of its incompleteness, the whole space is a strange mixture of the ornate and the austere, the gilt and the plain. The massive columns provide solidity, but the lack of a main *retablo* gives the church a pleasant sense of openness. There are many sculptures by Cano (who is buried in the crypt) and by Pedro de Mena, and Cano's masterpieces, a series of paintings of the life of the Virgin, hang around the cupola, but are helpfully reproduced around the ambulatory. It's a fine display of Spanish Baroque art, painted over a long period in the mid-17th century.

★Capilla Real

C Oficios s/n, T958-229239. Mon-Sat 1030-1315 and 1600-1915, Sun 1100-1315 and 1430-1745, hours vary slightly through year. €4.

If you have travelled a little in Spain, or read something of the nation's history, the very thought of viewing the tombs of the Catholic Monarchs, Fernando and Isabel,

ON THE ROAD
Granada Card

Granada's tourist pass costs €33.50 for the basic version and €37.50 for the 'plus' version. Both include entry to the Alhambra, Catedral, Capilla Real, Monasterio de la Cartuja, Monasterio de San Jerónimo and the Parque de las Ciencias, as well as being valid for five/nine journeys respectively by normal bus. The Plus card also allows one circuit in the tourist bus. It's not a huge saving. Buy it online at www.granadatur.com and pick it up at one of several places. At time of booking you'll have to reserve your time slot for the Alhambra. Some hotels give you one for free if you stay two nights or more, but you'll have to mention it when you check in.

who had such an impact on the world's history, might send an anticipatory shiver up your spine.

Although they had originally planned to be buried at Toledo, Fernando and Isabel decided in 1504 that it would be more fitting to rest in peace in Granada, symbolic scene of the triumph of their Catholic faith. Isabel died a few months later, in November of the same year, followed by Fernando (a pragmatic figure, once described by Shakespeare, accurately, as "reckon'd one the wisest prince that there had reign'd by many a year before") in 1516. Their bodies lay in the monastery (now parador) of San Francisco on the Alhambra hill until their grandson Carlos V could complete the chapel. He added a few modernizing touches to the Isabelline Gothic design, and brought their bodies here in 1521. By Fernando and Isabel's side, he also had tombs carved for his parents, Felipe El Hermoso (the Fair, who died in 1505), and Juana La Loca (the Mad), who was far from dead; she finally passed away in 1555, only three years before Carlos himself.

The burial chapel is entered through one of Carlos's additions to the original design, an inspirational Plateresque *reja* built by Bartolomé de Jaén between 1518 and 1520. Above depictions of the 12 apostles and the arms of Fernando and Isabel are scenes of the Passion and Resurrection of Christ.

The centre of the transept is occupied by the tombs themselves. Although you need to be incredibly tall to fully appreciate them, they are finely carved from Carrara marble. Fernando and Isabel are to the right as you enter, with Juana and Felipe beside them. The former tombs, notable for their realism, were carved by the Italian master Domenico Fancelli; the feet are guarded by tiny lions. Felipe and Juana are works of the Spaniard Bartolomé Ordóñez. An inscription reads: *Mahometice secte prostratores et heretice pervicacie extinctores* (Vanquishers of the Muslim sects and extinguishers of the lies of heretics). Descending a stair below the tombs you view the small crypt with its creepy lead coffins; there is also one for Fernando and Isabel's grandson, Miguel, who died in infancy. Ransacked by troops headed by Napoleon during the Peninsular War, it is doubtful whether the tombs now actually hold the monarchs' remains. The simplicity of the coffins reflects the austere faith of, in particular, Isabel, who desired to be buried unadorned.

The *retablo* is a suitably fine work, created in 1520-1522 by Felipe Vigarny, who was assisted by Jacobo of Florence and Alonso Berruguete among others.

The sacristy museum is entered through a doorway with a notable Isabelline Gothic flourish and an elegant Annunciation. The vaulted museum is fascinating, containing some royal standards and garments and Fernando's sword alongside the battered crown and sceptre of Isabel. Many of the queen's personal effects and paintings are also present, including some fine Flemish pieces, especially the masterly 15th-century *retablo* triptych by Bouts, featuring the Crucifixion, Descent, and Resurrection, and some exquisite Hans Memling paintings. There's also a work widely attributed to Botticelli as well as works by some Spanish masters.

Around the Capilla Real

Opposite the entrance to the Capilla Real is the cheerfully speckled façade of the **Palacio de la Madraza**, an old Islamic college (*madrassa*) now a university building. While the façade is post-Moorish, the building was constructed by the Nasrid king Yusuf I. Wander into the fine patio and examine the octagonal oratory with well-preserved Nasrid decorations adorning the walls, prayer niche and cupola. The colour is well preserved in parts, giving some idea of what the Alhambra palaces might have looked like centuries ago.

Across Calle Reyes Católicos, the **Corral del Carbón** ⓘ *entry fee due to be charged*, was once a Moorish inn, or *caravanserai*, where merchant convoys could hole up and store their goods. You enter the courtyard through a 14th-century arched portal decorated with *mocárabes*.

The **Ayuntamiento** on Plaza del Carmén also has a very fine patio; you're usually allowed to walk in and have a look.

Realejo and San Matías

This interesting zone, southeast of Plaza Nueva and running up the southern face of the Alhambra hill, was once home to much of the city's Jewish population. It's well worth a look, not least because it's still pretty local in character.

Plaza Mariana Pineda is a short walk from Puerta Real and is centred on a statue of the Granadan martyr whom Lorca immortalized in his play about her (see box, page 32). Near here, the **Iglesia de Santo Domingo** stands on a small square and has a high Renaissance portico reminiscent of the cathedral's western façade; the front of the church itself is covered in Romanizing frescoes. Further towards the Alhambra hill, the **Campo del Príncipe** is a large plaza cleared by the Catholic Monarchs to celebrate the wedding of their short-lived son. It's now a popular place for tapas.

Climbing up the hill with the orange-coloured Alhambra Palace hotel looming overhead, a side street leads to the **Casa Museo Manuel de Falla** ⓘ *Casa Museo: C Antequerela Alta 11, T958-228421, www.museomanueldefalla.com, Tue-Fri 0930-1800, Sat-Sun 0900-1400, Jul-Aug Wed-Sun 0900-1330, €3 (guided visit)*. De Falla (1876-1946) was a friend of Lorca's and Spain's most renowned composer. As well as writing *zarzuela* operas, he had a keen interest in flamenco. The *cante jondo* competition he organized in 1922 expressed his desire to revive a fast-disappearing art. The fairly humble *carmen* he lived in from 1921 has been lovingly preserved; much of the man's engaging, obsessive and hypochondriac character can be gleaned here thanks to the tour. Above the house is an exhibition on Falla and an auditorium that has regular live classical music.

Continuing from here past the **Alhambra Palace** hotel and down a narrow lane, you arrive at the Torres Bermejas (see La Alhambra, page 16).

Turning hairpin right at the Alhambra Palace and up the hill past the Falla auditorium brings you to the **Carmen de los Mártires** ① *Mon-Fri 1000-1400, 1600-1800 (1800-2000 summer), Sat and Sun 1000-1800 (2000 summer), free.* This extraordinary place consists of a decaying but opulent 19th-century palace surrounded by a lush and enormous park with various types of gardens. It's due for renovation, but it's a peaceful delight to wander the unkempt estate, finding unexpected fountains, sculptures and duckponds at every turn.

University district
north and west of the cathedral with several outstanding monuments

Hospital Real

Beyond the Puerta de Elvira, once the main gateway into the city, this endearing Renaissance building was commissioned by the Catholic Monarchs as a home for the mentally ill, an enlightened piece of work for those times. Completed by Carlos V, one of its early inmates was a young Portuguese called João, a former soldier who heard God tell him to care for the sick. After recovering from the shock of this, he was released from the madhouse and went about doing exactly that, founding a hospital of his own and becoming revered as a holy man. He is now known as San Juan de Dios, or John of God. If you are interested in his life, there's a small exhibition about him in the house where he died, Casa de los Pisa, in the Albayzín near Plaza Nueva.

Today the building is the main library of Granada's university, which is spread around this district. Set in a palm-filled garden, it features four patios, two of which are superbly harmonious examples of the purest Renaissance. In one of the others is a statue of Charles V, who founded the university.

Monasterio de San Jerónimo
C Gran Capitán s/n, T958-279337. Summer Mon-Fri 1000-1330, 1600-1930, Sat-Sun 1000-1430, 1600-1930, winter afternoons 1500-1830. €4.

Begun by the Catholic Monarchs four years after taking Granada, this monastery, the resting place of El Gran Capitán, Gonzalo de Córdoba, is especially notable for its vividly decorated church, much of which was designed by Diego de Siloé. The monastery suffered grievously at the hands of Napoleon's troops and, after the Disentailment Act of 1835, was used as a cavalry barracks, so it's something of a miracle that it's so well preserved today. It now has a population of 15 cloistered nuns. The cloister is a fine feature, with Renaissance arches offset by an Isabelline balustrade on the upper level. The capitals are worth examining; they are well carved with vegetal and mythical designs. There is an unusual loggia running alongside the church above the cloister level. After viewing some mediocre paintings in the refectory and chapterhouse, the church is like a fireworks display, decorated floor to ceiling with frescoes. One of the artists went berserk with a cherub gun; it would take all day to count how many of the winged innocents there are. The painted side chapels feature scenes from history and lives of the saints, while the huge dusty gold *retablo* (worth a coin to light it up) is dedicated to the Immaculate Conception; its panels feature scenes of Mary's life. In one of the chapels, note Pedro de Mena's fine sculpture of Nuestra Señora de la Soledad; one of Granada's favourites of the Semana Santa processions at Easter. Note the elaborate vaulting, the cupola over the crossing abuzz with cherubs and busts, and the separate gallery and choir for the nuns. The tomb of Gonzalo is before the high altar; the church was completed by his wife to provide a suitable resting place for the great soldier. Statues of the couple at prayer flank the *retablo*.

Monasterio de la Cartuja
Paseo de Cartuja s/n, T958-161932. Daily 1000-1300, 1600-2000 (1500-1800 winter), €4. Bus No 8 will get you here from Gran Vía, or a 30-min walk from the centre, or take the LAC bus westwards and change to the N7.

This former Carthusian monastery merits a visit for its riotous Baroque church. A construction project plagued with problems, the building was commenced in the early 16th century but not completely finished until the monks were booted out by the Disentailment Act of 1835. Walking around the cloister you can sense the austere hard-working, contemplative lives of the 'white robes', and the vaulted chapterhouse features paintings of historical persecutions inflicted on the monks. All of which adds to the contrast that awaits when entering the church, which is a dazzling array of the colourful and the flamboyant.

The nave is divided into three sections; one for the public, one for the lay-brothers, and one for the monks. The last two were separated by an elaborate tortoiseshell door paned with Venetian glass; it's placed in a Baroque screen decorated with canvases by Sánchez Cotón, just two of many fine paintings in here. The choir stalls have beautiful mouldings around them, while the walls in general are covered with polychrome plasterwork. A gilt baldachin sits over the altar and features the Assumption of the Virgin; above is a cupola with well-rendered cherubs peering down on the bewildered visitor. Behind it, a glassed arch leads to the Sanctuary Chapel. The dome and walls are painted by Palomino, who also did much work in Córdoba's cathedral, but the room is dominated by an immense tabernacle in the centre. The whole is a gilt and marble fantasy, executed to perfection, and, once in here, it's decision time: love it or hate it. After this, no visitor could possibly have mixed feelings about Spanish Baroque.

The sacristy is also exceptionally ornamental, but here the straight line has been eschewed, giving the extraordinary sensation that the room is melting, a feeling partly brought about by the unusual Alpujarran marble, which has streaks of colour that make it look like an exotic chocolate cocktail. There are a pair of sculptures of St Bruno, one of the founders of the Carthusian order, and an 18th-century painted dome.

★There are three museums in and around Granada set up in houses where Federico García Lorca (see box, page 32) once lived.

The first is now in the city itself, but was once a summer house outside town, in the fertile meadows known as La Vega. This is the **Casa Museo de Federico García Lorca** ⓘ *T958-258466, Tue-Sun 0915-1330, 1715-1930 or 1600-1830, closed afternoons mid-Jun to mid-Sep, garden 0800-dusk, tours (mandatory) on the half-hour, €3, free on Wed*. Lorca's father bought it in 1925, when it was a small farmhouse among other such properties. From the age of 27 until his death at 38, Lorca spent most of his summers here and produced much of his best work in the place, which he loved dearly. With the help of Lorca's late sister Isabel, the house has been returned to its original state. Very modern for its time, it's now an interesting period piece. By far the most fascinating part is Lorca's bedroom and writing desk. In the room hangs a Rafael Alberti painting; downstairs is a sketch by Salvador Dalí, who was a very close friend of Lorca's, and a famous portrait by Toledo of the poet in a yellow dressing gown, a typically humorous touch on his part. Lorca's joy for life is tangible in the small remnants of his existence here.

The second museum, **Museo Casa-Natal Federico García Lorca** ⓘ *T958-516453, www.museogarcialorca.org, visits on the hour Oct-Mar Tue-Sun 1000-1300, 1600-1700 Apr-Jun 1000-1300, 1700-1800, Jul-Sep 1000-1400, €1.80*, is in a village 17 km west of Granada called Fuente Vaqueros, surrounded by lands that once belonged to the Duke of Wellington. This is where Lorca was born in 1898 and lived his early years. The house has been painstakingly recreated as it was in those days. The tour will show you the kitchen and bedrooms, including drawings by young Federico that were made into embroidery by his sister, copies of his birth and baptismal certificates, and school photos. Upstairs, the granary has been converted into an exhibition room, while across the grapevine-covered courtyard is another room where you can see video footage of the man himself. Although simple, it's an excellent museum, largely due to the tour being conducted by a man with a deep love for and knowledge of the poet.

To get there by car, exit Granada on the Málaga–Antequera road and, as you pass the airport, take the exit for Fuente Vaqueros. Turning right at the roundabout in the centre of the village, the house is signposted on the left. Buy tickets at the rear, on the parallel street. Buses leave Granada from Avenida de Andaluces by the train station hourly (except 1000) on weekdays, and at 0900, 1100, 1300, 1700, 1900 and 2100 at weekends. Return buses leave Fuente an hour later. The journey takes 20 minutes.

Another site is just outside the village of **Alfacar** north of Granada (regular buses from Calle Capitán Moreno in Granada, next to the Arco de Elvira arch), where the poet was shot in August 1936. A rather unpoetic memorial park has been built on the spot, but the olive tree where he is said to have died and been buried, though his remains were not found there in a recent excavation, is a more sobering place indeed and worth the journey.

ON THE ROAD

The poet they silenced

One of Spain's finest writers, the poet and dramatist Federico García Lorca was born in 1898 at Fuente Vaqueros, near Granada, to a prosperous farmer and former local schoolteacher. While studying law none too enthusiastically at Granada, he published his first book of poems; at the same time he got to know the composer Manuel de Falla and became an accomplished musician. He then went to study in Madrid, meeting important contemporaries, such as Salvador Dalí, Pablo Neruda, and Juan Ramón Jiménez. Lorca developed a deep interest in Andalucían life and culture and had an enduring passion for gypsy life and flamenco. By the age of 30, he had achieved national fame for a play, *Mariana Pineda*, based on the exploits of Granada's 19th-century liberal martyr, and his book of gypsy ballads, *Romancero Gitano*. *Poema del Cante Jondo* was a long lyric poem that also captured the flamenco mood.

On the strength of the success of *Romancero Gitano*, Lorca went to live in New York for a year, learning English and writing the depressed and alienated poems that were to appear after his death as *Poeta en Nueva York*. On his return to Spain, he ran a popular travelling theatre for the Republican government; in these years he produced his best-known stage works *Bodas de Sangre* (Blood Wedding), *Yerma* and *La Casa de Bernarda Alba*, all dealing with passions, emotions and the female condition in rural Spain. In 1935, his poem *Llanto por Ignacio Sánchez Mejías* (Lament for the Death of a Bullfighter), an elegy for the great *torero* and friend of Lorca's who was gored in the ring in Manzanares in 1934, won great critical acclaim.

Lorca spent as much of his time in Granada as he could, but was openly critical of the city's middle classes, who he labelled as uncultured boors. This attitude, together with his Republican sympathies and his homosexuality, were to see him seized from the house of a Falangist friend shortly after the Civil War started, detained and then driven to the village of Viznar by a group of fascist thugs acting for the military governor. On the morning of 19 or 20 August 1936, he was driven outside the village and forced to dig his own grave by an olive tree. He was then shot several times, a deed which the perpetrators later boasted about in Granada. His books were burned in the town square and were soon banned by Franco. Despite renewed efforts to find his grave in recent years, body has never been identified among the thousands killed.

Lorca's Granada, by biographer Ian Gibson (Faber and Faber, 1992) is a labour of love that leads you on a series of walks through Granada, pointing out spots where Lorca lived, ate and drank and that he wrote about, all the while filling you in with fascinating background information on his life and excerpts of his poetry.

Nearby, on the edge of the village, is a spot to clear your thoughts somewhat; the **Fuente Grande**, a natural spring whose combination of clear water and green plants is somehow intensely satisfying. Watch for the bubbles naturally bursting to the surface; the Moors named the site 'the fountain of tears'.

Other Lorca sites you may like to visit in Granada include **Chikito** restaurant (detailed below) where he used to chat with a group of friends, the hotel **Alhambra Palace** (see below) where he performed readings, Falla's house nearby, where he was a frequent visitor, and the hotel **Reina Cristina** ⓘ *C Tablas 4*. This used to be the residence of the poet Luis Rosales, and it was where Lorca was snatched from in the early days of the Civil War before being driven outside Granada to his murder; however, it's changed much since those days. Unfortunately another of his favourite cafés, the **Gran Café Granada** on Puerta Real, is these days a Burger King.

Listings Granada city *maps p12, p16 and p22*

Tourist information

Tourist office
C Santa Ana 4, T958-225990, otgranada@andalucia.org. Mon-Fri 0900-1930, Sat and Sun 0930-1500.
The city's handiest office is just off Plaza Nueva. The provincial tourist office (Plaza de Mariana Pineda 10, T958-247128, Mon-Fri 0900-2000 (1900 in winter), Sat 1000-1900, Sun 1000-1500) is larger and less crowded. Both have a good information on transport, accommodation and opening hours of sights (which change frequently), as well as city maps and information about the province. Within the Alhambra ticket pavilion is another tourist office; there are also various kiosks around town that are closed in winter. Look for the free guide *Guía de Granada*; a useful monthly 'what's on' publication.

Where to stay

Granada has a huge range of accommodation options, with hundreds of hotels and *pensiones*. Apart from a couple of recommendable hotels around (and in) the Alhambra itself, the choicest and most romantic area to stay is the old Moorish quarter of the Albayzín, where several superbly renovated mansion-hotels offer patios, beamed rooms and Alhambra views. There's a huge concentration of budget accommodation in the university zone, around C San Juan de Dios, so head there if there are no rooms around Plaza Nueva.

The tourist office and various online resources can provide a list of apartments for rent; also look out for signs around the city, particularly near the Albayzín.

La Alhambra

€€€€ Alhambra Palace
C Peña Partida 2, T958-221468, www.h-alhambrapalace.es.
This huge orange castellated affair is far from subtle, and caused much controversy when it was built in 1910 on the Alhambra hill. That said, once you're inside you can forget about the slightly gauche exterior and concentrate on the luxury of the rooms and installations and

the superb views of the city or Alhambra, depending on which side your room is. The bar's terrace is one of Granada's prime spots for a drink; there's also a good restaurant and a small theatre where Lorca recited poetry a few times. Extras like breakfast are expensive.

€€€€ Parador San Francisco
Real de la Alhambra s/n, T958-221440, www.parador.es.
With comparatively few rooms, however, booking well in advance is essential; think at least several months in peak periods. This is Spain's flagship parador, with an enviable location within the Alhambra complex itself. Built as a monastery by the Catholic Monarchs, it's a magnificent nexus of luxury and history. Bear in mind that you are paying a premium for location here.

€€€ Carmen de la Alcubilla del Caracol
Aire Alta 12, T958-215551, www. alcubilladel caracol.com. Closed Aug.
In a very secluded location on the side of the Alhambra hill below the Torres Bermejas, this boutique hotel doesn't exactly trip off the tongue but has 7 gorgeous rooms, some with balconies overlooking town. It's a lovely traditional Granada *carmen* with a beautiful spacious interior enlivened by thoughtfully selected furniture. Service is warm and personal and numerous caring touches make for a memorable stay. Recommended.

€€€ Hotel América
Real de la Alhambra 53, T958-227471, www.hotelamericagranada.com. Closed Dec-Feb. Booking well in advance is crucial.
Right in the Alhambra, this small hotel doesn't only deliver on location. Set around a vine-covered patio café, it exudes character from every pore; from the creaky wooden staircase decorated with paintings to the snug venerable rooms furnished with rustic vintage sofas and (narrow) beds. It's far from luxurious but intensely charismatic. You have to go elsewhere for meals and park in the Alhambra car park.

Plaza Nueva to Sacromonte

€€ Cuevas El Abanico
Verea de Enmedio 89, T958-226199, T608-848497, www.el-abanico.com. Reservation advisable; minimum stay of 3 nights in busy periods.
A must for those with troglodyte tendencies, these smartly appointed cave apartments are in the heart of Sacromonte. The standard cave is long, white and decorated with tiles and other Andalucían favourites. There's a well-equipped kitchen, bathroom and a bedroom annex. And blankets, as the caves are a cool 18°C all year. You can't park very close, so it's not for those who don't fancy lugging bags. Recommended.

€ Hostal Navarro Ramos
Cuesta de Gomérez 21, T958-250555, www.pension navarroramos.com.
Family-run place whose simple tiled-floored and white-walled rooms are well looked after. Like all the places on this hill, the rooms on the street are very noisy. Priced very low; the shared bathrooms have good showers. Centrally heated in winter. Recommended.

El Albayzín

€€€ Casa Morisca
Cuesta de la Victoria 9, T958-221100, www.hotelcasamorisca.com.
A late 15th-century home in the Albayzín just off the picturesque

Paseo de los Tristes, this sumptuous and intimate hotel exudes charm and neo-Moorish grace. A delightful pool in the central patio is surrounded by restored a restored wooden gallery; the rooms and passageways feature inlaid ceilings returned to their original glory. The rooms on the street are especially desirable, but all are classily and comfortably furnished in the same style as the rest of the building. It's usually possible to park in the street outside. Recommended.

€€€ El Ladrón de Agua
Carrera del Darro 13, T958-215040, www.ladrondeagua.com.
One of several gloriously refurbished historic Albayzín houses, this hotel is among the best. The rooms are lovely, but not overburdened decoratively – they let the attractive brick, tile and wood surfaces create the harmony. As in all these hotels, there are many distinct types and prices of rooms, some quite small, others rather luxurious. There's a literary theme to the rooms here, with each named after a work by Lorca or Juan Ramón Jiménez. Meals are also available for guests.

€€€ Hotel Casa 1800
C Benalúa 11, T958-210700, www. hotelcasa1800granada.com.
This handsome lodging has become one of Granada's most appealing hotels. The rooms, surrounding a typically elegant patio, are romantic and attractively decorated in a sober style. The location is excellent, and some superior rooms have views of the Alhambra. Service is great, and there are loads of thoughtful extras, though no on-site parking. Recommended.

€€ Hotel Santa Isabel la Real
C Santa Isabel la Real 19, T958-294658, www.hotel santaisabellareal.com.
Set in our favourite part of the Albayzín, just off Plaza San Miguel Bajo, this small hotel has a fine, peaceful location by the convent of the same name. With very attractive rooms around a light central patio, helpful staff, and a couple of great restaurants nearby, it's a top option. Very handily, bus C1 stops outside the door. Breakfast included. Recommended.

€ Oasis Backpackers' Hostel
Placeta Correo Viejo 3, T958-215848, www.oasisgranada.com.
This excellent backpackers' hostel is tucked away in the Albayzín, not far from C de Elvira. Exceedingly well run, it offers all the comforts and luxuries a traveller could hope for. Accommodation is in clean and comfortable dorms (doubles also available), and you get your own personal safe – a great feature. There's a lively social scene here, with a roof terrace (top views) and a good kitchen available 24/7. Recommended.

The Catedral and around

€€€€ Hospes Palacio de los Patos
C Solarillo de Gracia 1, T958-535790, www.hospes.com.
Occupying an exquisite 19th-century mansion in the heart of Granada, this 5-star choice has an excellent central location but the quiet and relaxation of a rural hotel. The pretty garden and classy restaurant are complemented by most elegant interior decoration and chic white modern rooms.

€€€ Hotel Palacio de los Navas
C Navas 1, T958-215760, www. palaciodelosnavas.com.

This excellent boutique hotel, set in a 16th-century *mudéjar palacio*, is a real treat at the end of this excellent tapas street. The rooms, of which there are 2 categories, are a little dark but very pleasant and comfortable, and the elegant building, constructed around a pretty patio, is most appealing. The staff are great, and the whole place is kept absolutely spotless, especially the praiseworthy bathrooms. One room has disabled access.

€€ Hotel Las Nieves
C Alhóndiga 8, T958-265311, www. hotellasnieves.com.
A professional and friendly choice in the shopping zone, and handy for just about everything, this has warmly decorated modern rooms with excellent bathrooms. Staff are helpful and prices are particularly attractive; off-season, staying here offers exceptional value. There's a restaurant with a decent *menú*.

€€ Hotel Párragasiete
C Párraga 7, T958-264227, www. hotelparragasiete.com.
This boutique hotel is on a quiet street but is very central. Rooms offer plenty of style and comfortable beds; they include decent singles. There's also a restaurant with gastronomic pretensions. Recommended.

€ Hostal Costa Azul
C Rosario T958-222298, www. hostalcostaazul.com.
This unassuming spot is perfectly situated for sallies forth to the tapas heartland of C Navas, and has a pretty tiled patio, little garden, free Wi-Fi and laundry service. It's a friendly spot, but try not to get shunted across the road to the annexe, where rooms aren't as inviting.

Camping

Camping Sierra Nevada
C Juan Pablo II 23, T958-150062, www.campingsierranevada.com. Mar-Oct. Bus SN2 runs from here to a connection with the central LAC service.
A well-equipped campsite near the bus station in a perfect location. The pool is a godsend in the summer heat. Recommended.

Restaurants

The highlight of Granada's eating scene is its tapas culture. Bars here charge more for drinks, but give free tapas with each, giving different tapas for each round of drinks.

Boisterous C de Elvira just off Plaza Nueva is a popular place to start your tapas trail, but prices are high and you'll find more tourists than locals. C Navas is the favourite for many *granadinos*. The plazas of the Albayzin have sunkissed terraces for alfresco snacking, and the university district has numerous good-value tapas choices and a convivial studenty atmosphere.

Among Granada's restaurants are a selection of mirador eateries with superb views of the Alhambra. The city is well stocked with *teterías*, atmospheric teahouses serving minty Moroccan tea and other infusions, waterpipes and Maghrebi pastries.

Remember that Granada sees a huge number of tourists. Beware any place without prices marked on its menus and always check prices on terraces before ordering.

Plaza Nueva to Sacromonte

€€ La Taberna de Tiacheta
Puente Cabrera s/n.
This bar is romantically set by an old bridge over the river. It's a small set-up with a friendly feel and excellent tapas; try the *morcilla* if you're a fan of blood sausage, or choose from a number of other thoughtfully prepared deli-style plates.

€€ Ruta del Azafrán
Paseo Padre Manjón 1, T958 226 882, www.rutadelazafran.es.
With a lovely setting on Paseo de los Tristes, and views up to the Alhambra from the outdoor tables, this makes a romantic dinner spot. Many dishes are Moroccan-influenced, and portions are healthy rather than hearty, but it's all tasty and served with a smile.

Cafés

Heladería Tiggiani
C Cuchilleros 15, T958-252811.
On Plaza Nueva, this wonderful ice creamery delights with its beautifully presented concoctions, with flavours like Ferrero Rocher or Cointreau. Another branch on Plaza Bib-Rambla.

El Albayzín *map p12*
The Albayzín is fertile ground for tapas, particularly during the day, and has a selection of classy restaurants, many offering Alhambra views. The streets around C de Elvira form the classic tapas zone, but it's often crowded and touristy.

€€€ Mirador de Aixa
Carril de San Agustín 2, T958-223616, www.miradordeaixa.com. Closed Sun night and Mon.
There are several mirador restaurants in the Albayzín, most with wonderful views across to the Alhambra and attractive places to eat by day or night, when the complex is floodlit. In some, you pay mostly for location, but this is one of the better options, just below the Mirador de San Nicolás. The menu is short in length and high on quality, from a delicious house *revuelto* to a sizeable *chuletón* steak; Moorish-inspired dishes like aubergines with honey are a less carnivorous option. Service is friendly, and the terrace is prettily covered with vines.

€€ El Ají
Plaza San Miguel Bajo 9, T958-292930, www.restauranteelaji.com.
This warmly decorated and friendly place has quickly become a favourite with Albayzín locals, who already have several good options on this square. It's modern, but cheerfully so, and this extends to the food, which is thoughtfully concocted and presented. There are vegetarian choices, including good salads, as well as tasty grilled meats. The *menú* is good and low priced, but à la carte is even better. There are outdoor tables.

€€ Taberna Salinas
C de Elvira 13, T958-221411, www.tabernassalinas.com.
This is touristy but has an old-fashioned cavernous bodega atmosphere with hams hanging over the bar and is dimly lit and cosy. The plates that accompany the drinks for free here are excellent, and there are plenty of tables where you can dine on a wide choice of classic tapas and *raciones*.

€ Antigua Bodegas Castañeda
C Almireceros 3, T958-223222.
This long-established classy joint serves classic tapas dishes such as *cazuelas* (stews) as well as mixed plates of cured

meats and cheeses. Stepping inside recalls a bygone age. It's always packed; locals enjoy its large selection of barrelled wines. Try the *calicasa*, a potent blend of vermouth and other goodies, which is tasty and strong. There's a newer but equally popular version of the same bar behind it. Not really recommended for a sit-down meal though.

€ Bar Aixa
Plaza Larga 5.
On this appealing square tucked up the back of the Albayzín, this typical local tapas bar stands out for its big-hearted service, democratic feel, and generous free tapas. Try a *ración* of potatoes or snails on the terrace.

€ Bar León
C Pan 1, www.restaurante barleon.com.
Much more authentic and down-to-earth than most of the bars in the Elvira zone, this has tasty traditional raciones from all around Spain, including such will-I-won't-I delicacies as *sesos* (brains) and *criadillas* (bull testicles), as well as fried fish and *callos* (tripe). It's a welcoming haven of Granada normality.

€ Bodega La Mancha
C Joaquín Costa 10, T958-228968.
A wonderfully traditional spot around the corner from the C de Elvira action and a world away from it. It's a gruffly welcoming, handsome, proper Spanish bar that does cracking tortilla and serves up a range of no-nonsense wines to go with it. They don't usually give a free tapa, but there's a range of cheap ones to choose from – try their tasty *croquetas* (croquettes) or excellent tortilla.

€ Puerta de las Pesas
Plaza Larga s/n.
With a great little terrace right by an impressive Moorish gateway, this is one of the better spots to stop off for a drink and a bite while strolling around the Albayzín. The tiny bar itself is warmly decorated and run by a family. It's not flash, but it's honest, friendly and authentic.

€ Taberna el 22
Cuesta de San Gregorio 5.
A small and hospitable bar with a popular terrace on the way up into the Albayzín. The tapas are fabulous, as are the cheap *raciones*: *revuelto de setas* (scrambled eggs with wild mushrooms) is just one of many changing and recommended choices, with lots of vegetarian options. Try the orange wine too; a curious Andalucían beverage that's very tasty – at least for the first glass.

Cafés
Rising off C de Elvira, C Calderería Nueva is like stepping into a Moroccan souk. There are several atmospheric teahouses, all with comfortable low seating, ambient North African music, and a fine range of teas served in exquisite pots. Everyone has their personal favourite, but they are all good.

The Catedral and around
C Navas off Plaza del Carmen is a pedestrian street almost wholly devoted to bars, many of them excellent.

€€€ Carmen San Miguel
Plaza Torres Bermejas 3, T958-226723, www.carmen sanmiguel.com.
Closed Sun.
Right by the Torres Bermejas, this secluded restaurant offers a covered terrace with unbeatable views over the city in a traditional *carmen* where the Russian composer Glinka once lived while studying Spanish musical forms in the 19th century. The menu won't

disappoint either; the chef produces creations of great originality and taste. Their vanilla roasted suckling pig is a signature dish.

€€€ Damasqueros
C Damasqueros 3, T958-210550, www.damasqueros.com.
The 5-course degustation menu here (€42) changes weekly and combines both sensational local ingredients with imaginative presentation. A reasonably priced wine flight is offered alongside. Don't confuse with the bar of the same name on the corner of this street. Recommended.

€€€-€€ Chikito
Plaza del Campillo 9, T958-223364, www.restaurantechikito.com. Closed Wed.
In Lorca's day this was a café, and he used to spend much time in discussion here with friends sitting in a corner; the group thus became known as *El Rinconcillo*. Although it's now a restaurant, one senses the poet would have approved of the warm-coloured dining room hung with photos of Lorca himself and of other famous visitors. A dish the house prides itself upon is its *zarzuela* (casserole) of fish and seafood; in fact the fish dishes here tend to shine brighter than the meat ones; there's a Basque touch to many of the offerings. Book ahead if possible, as it's a long-standing local favourite.

€€€ Vinoteca Puerta del Carmen
Plaza del Carmen 1, T958-223737, www.puerta delcarmenrestaurante.com.
A favourite of the well-dressed *funcionarios* from the town hall opposite, this bar features an excellent selection of fine Spanish wines, helpful service, and tapas and *raciones* of deli products, including excellent ham and *salazones*

(salted fish preserves). There are pleasant tables outside on the terrace and an elegant interior.

€€ Casa Enrique
C Acera de Darro 8, T958-255008, www.tabernacasaenrique.es.
Open since 1911, this is a deserved local favourite nicknamed El Elefante perhaps because it's so small. Decked out with dark wood, hanging hams and old wine bottles, and without a seat in the place, it's a classic Spanish bar and has heaps of atmosphere. There are deli products from all over Spain; like Jabugo ham, Galician cheese, Burgos *morcilla* or Bierzo chorizo. There's also tasty house vermouth from the barrel. Tapas are not free here. Highly recommended.

€€ La Brujidera
C Monjas del Carmen 2, T958-202595.
A dark and atmospheric venue with one of the city's best selections of wines by the glass. Work your way through the regions of Spain; the bartender will be happy to give advice on some of the lesser known choices such as Ribeiro, Somontano and Bierzo. These all come well accompanied; the bar specializes in ham and chorizo, and there are tempting mixed platters of pâtés and cheeses available, and some seriously delicious ciabattas, as well as the mouth-watering queen scallops, *zamburiñas*. Draws a loyal Granada crowd who never tire of discussing the significant merits of Spanish food and wine. Tough to find (the name isn't prominent), but worth the effort. Recommended.

€€ Rossini
Campo del Príncipe 15, T686-312118.
An equally good choice for tapas or a full meal, the warm fern-filled interior of this busy and stylish eatery is redolent with

the aromas of cheeses. There's a large range of these, as well as pâtés, smoked fish and cured meats and hams (the latter particularly appropriate as Rossini was addicted to hams from nearby Trevélez). Order *raciones* of 100 g or so, or opt for a large mixed dish.

€ Bodegas Espadafor
Gran Vía 59, T958-202138.
Steeped in tradition, this bar is more than a century old and doesn't seem to have changed much. It's a fabulous spot, a big bodega with their own wine served from barrels, tiles on the walls, *raciones* and tapas of things like cooked ham that really hit the spot, and a patina of generations of contented customers.

€ Hicuri
C Santa Escolástica 4, T858-987473.
This cheerily colourful place is a sound breakfast stop, then puts on delicious non-typical vegetarian and vegan food. Staff are friendly, there's an emphasis on organic produce, and there are some great desserts.

University district
Southwest of the centre, this area bristles with good-value tapas bars that serve a populous residential area as well as students. Plaza Einstein, a couple of blocks west of the D1 square of our map, is the hub, off which run the tapas-rich streets of C Gonzalo Gallas and C Pintor López Mezquita. Parallel C Sol is another with plenty of choice.

€€ Botánico
C Málaga 3, T958-271598, www. botanicocafe.es.
A polished, modern spacious café-restaurant that offers a bit of everything: coffees on its terrace by the small botanical gardens, late-night weekend

DJ sessions, but, above all, fantastic food. The menu is avant-garde for Granada, and always features a range of interesting daily specials. There's a lot of vegetarian choice; dishes with tofu or fried goat's cheese take their place alongside meatier things like quail rice or an excellent roast duck. Service is efficient and welcoming, the house Rioja excellent and the atmosphere warm. Recommended.

Granada suburbs
A popular tapas zone that few tourists get to is in the residential suburb of La Chana, just off the Ctra de Málaga in the northwest of the city. There are several bars here in a block known as Las Torres, all with terraces that are popular at weekends. The key factor is that to get people to make the effort to come out here, the free tapas have to be high quality and large – and they are. All the streets here are named after fish; there are enough bars here to make it worth the taxi ride.

Bars and clubs

Granada has excellent nightlife – for year-round reliability it's just about Andalucía's best – including on week nights, when a mix of students and tourists keep things pumping. C de Elvira is an excellent street for bars; the university zone around C Duquesa is fertile ground, and there's a high concentration of weekend bars around C Pedro Antonio de Alarcón and its intersections with C Socrates, C Emperatriz, C Eugenia and C Pintor López Mezquita. Grab vouchers from the people on the street outside the bars for cheaper drinks.

El Albayzín

El Enano Rojo
C de Elvira 91.
One of Granada's best bars, this smoky den is a reliable standby on a night out, being open from 2200 until 0300 on weekdays and 0400 at weekends. The music played depends on the whim of the bar staff, but it centres around 1980s and 1990s alternative rock. The crowd is an appropriate mix of students and people who bought the original singles.

The Catedral and around

Café Pícaro
C Varela 10, T619-203616.
Daily 1600-0300.
Run by a local writer, this is a smart, popular spot with good chat, a relaxing vibe, and regular live jazz. It's handy for a coffee or a *copa* after a visit to the C Navas tapas zone.

La Estrella
C Cuchilleros 7.
A major star in the Granada bar firmament, this dark tunnel-like place tucked away not far from Plaza Nueva has absolutely no pretensions except those to being one of the best bars in the city. A real mix of people and music, and open late every night. Just the ticket for those looking to lurk in an authentic atmosphere. No sign, but the blue neon star marks the spot.

Loop
C San Matías 8.
Popular for a *copa* after tapas on C Navas, this small spot bustles at weekends thanks to its hospitable bar staff and cool white-tiled bar. If you like the music, you can buy it – a wall of vinyl albums hangs for sale behind the bar.

Verdi
C Sacristía de San Matías 18.
Open from 2200 to 0200.
Look behind the San Matías church for this elegantly baroque bar, a quiet, refined little place run by a guy who believes in the art of cocktail making. It's unusual and a great spot for a secluded drink with someone special. Recommended.

Entertainment

Bullfights
There are regular bullfights at **Plaza de Toros** northwest of town, but especially important during Corpus Christi. The box office is on C Escudo del Carmen, open evenings only, when a fight is imminent. You can book tickets in advance on www.mundotoro.com.

Cinemas
Multicines Centro, C Solarillo de Gracia 9, T958-252950, www.multicines-centro.com. The closest of the multiplexes to town.

Flamenco
The Sacromonte area is filled with touristy flamenco shows, in which visitors pay €20-30 for a drink and a performance, with bus transport available for a few extra euros. Though certainly not for aficionados, there can be a good atmosphere, with busloads of tourists being invited up on stage to try a bit of dancing or clapping.

Much better than those, however, are: La Alboreá, *C Pan 3, T664-362540, www.liveflamencoshow.com.* Tucked away just off Plaza Nueva, this offers 2 decent shows nightly for €20. **Casa del Arte Flamenco**, *Cuesta de Gomérez 11, T958-565767,* www.casadelarteflamenco.com. 2 decent-quality shows nightly in a handy central location. Entry €18.

Peña la Platería, *Placeta de Toqueros 7, T958-210650, www.laplateria.org.es.* A long-established flamenco social club in the Albayzín. While it's officially members-only for the Sat night show, you may get in if you show interest; otherwise it's the public Thu night show for €8. It starts at 2230 and runs from Oct to Jun.

Zambra María la Canastera, *Camino del Sacromonte 89, T958-121183, www.maria lacanastera.com.* In Sacromonte, but more professional and intimate than most, €22. Show at 2200 nightly, 2145 in winter.

Theatre

The central **Teatro Isabel la Católica**, C Almona del Campillo 2, T958-221514, www.teatroisabellacatolica.es, is the main theatre. **Auditorio Manuel de Falla**, Paseo de los Mártires s/n, T958-221144, www.manueldefalla.org, has frequent classical concerts.

Festivals

1-2 Jan Día de la Toma, when the reconquest of Granada is celebrated with official processions, while the townsfolk queue up to ring the bell on the Alhambra's Torre de la Vela – tradition has it that any single girl doing so will be engaged within the year.

1st Sun in Feb To celebrate the **Fiesta of San Cecilio**, a *romería* (pilgrimage walk) winds its way up into Sacromonte.

Easter Semana Santa, traditional Holy Processions throughout the week, on a smaller scale to Sevilla or Córdoba but well attended nonetheless. The highlight is the Sat night, when Nuestra Señora de las Angustias is paraded within the Alhambra precinct.

Jun Corpus Christi, Granada's major fiesta, with street parties, bullfights, fireworks and a *feria* in the Almanjayour district in the west of town. The celebrations last 9 days centred on the Thu itself: 4 Jun 2015, 26 May 2016, 15 Jun 2017, 31 May 2018.

Jun/Jul International Festival of Music and Dance (www.granadafestival.org), in various locations in the city.

Last Sun of Sep Fiesta of Nuestra Señora de las Angustias, with bullfights and a procession.

1st 2 weeks in Nov International Jazz Festival (www.jazzgranada.es).

Shopping

Clothes

The main region for clothes shopping is at the top of C Recogidas and the streets around, while **El Corte Inglés** on C Acera del Darro is a well-stocked department store.

Guitars

There are several guitar-makers around the old town, including **Casa Morales**, Cuesta de Gomérez 9, T958-221387.

Souvenirs

Granada abounds in souvenir shops, but not all can be written off as tacky. Many sell ornate Granadan marquetry work, typically jewellery boxes and chess sets, and Spanish and Moorish-style ceramics. C Calderería Nueva, C de Elvira and the streets around have a range of Moroccan-style products, from *chichas/* hookahs to tea sets and slippers. Another area, southeast of the cathedral around Pasaje Zacatín off Plaza Bib-Rambla, has developed into a pretty authentic souk and is well worth a look.

What to do

Baths

Hammam, *C Santa Ana 16, T958-229978, granada.hammamalandalus.com.* A luxuriously appointed Arab bathhouse, whose decoration will take you right back to the glory years of Moorish Granada. With hot- and cold-water pools and optional massage, it's a perfect way to relax. Entry is by 2-hr time slot; it's advisable to book a day or so ahead (by phone, in person or online). Daily 1000-2400; bath only €24, bath plus massage €36, discounts and offers available online.

Bike and scooter hire

Ecoway, *Plaza Cuchilleros 6, T672-228890, www.ecowayrental.com.* Hire bikes from €19 a day at a convenient central location just off Plaza Nueva.

Language schools

There are dozens of Spanish schools in Granada. All offer accommodation arrangements in host families and a range of cultural activities. Some to try are:
Carmen de las Cuevas, Calle Cueste de los Chinos 15, T958-221062, www.carmencuevas.com. **DeLengua**, Calle Calderería Vieja 20, T958-204535, www.delengua.es. **Escuela Montalbán**, Calle Conde Cifuentes 11, T958-256875, www.escuela-montalban.com. **Instituto Europeo**, Calle Marqués de Mondéjar 40, T958-535760, www.e-institutoeuropeo.com. Calle San Antón 72, T958-010172, www.shm.edu. **Spanish Abroad**, www.spanishabroad.com. 2-week immersion language courses.

Tours

Cicerone, *T607-691676, www.cicerone granada.com.* Walking tours of Granada leave from the kiosk on Plaza Bib-Rambla, they cost €15 (under-14s free). They leave twice daily; there are separate Spanish and English groups. The tour takes about 2½ hrs and doesn't take in the Alhambra except at a distance. There's no need to book.

There's the inevitable **hop-on, hop-off red bus tour** that does 2 circuits, 1 around the new town (including the Alhambra) in a double decker, and 1 around the Albayzín and Alhambra in a minibus.

From a kiosk on Plaza Nueva near the Cuesta de Gomérez, you can rent an audio guide, **This.Is:Granada**, www.thisis.ws, covering a total of 4 different walking routes, including the Alhambra and Albayzín. It comes with 2 sets of headphones so a couple can listen simultaneously, and has commentary in several languages with a mildly annoying soundtrack. €15 for 5 days.

Transport

Air

Granada's airport, named after Lorca, is 17 km west of town. Buses run between the airport and the centre to coincide with flights, stopping on Acera del Darro, near the cathedral, and at the bus station door, 40 mins, €3, T958-490164, www.autocaresjosegonzalez.com.

There are daily flights from Granada's airport to **Madrid** and **Barcelona**, and regular flights to a couple of other domestic destinations as well as a **British Airways** service to **London City**.

Bus

The bus station is a long way from the centre of town, on Ctra de Jaén; a 30-min walk, or take a cab and a combination of buses.

For bus information, T900-710900. **Alsa** (www.alsa.es) is one of the main operators.

Granada is well connected by road with the rest of Andalucía.

Within Granada province, regular daily buses run from here to the coast at **Motril** (1 hr 20 mins) and **Salobreña/ Almuñécar** (1 hr 15 mins/1 hr 30 mins).

There are 6-9 daily buses to **Orgiva** (1 hr 15 mins) via Lanjarón, the gateway to the **Alpujarras** (45 mins); 2 of these continue further to **Ugijar** and outlying villages. **Güejar-Sierra** has 10 buses on weekdays, but less at weekends (25 mins), while **Guadix** (1 hr 30 mins) and **Montefrío** are served almost hourly on weekdays but only a couple of times on Sun.

There are 3 daily buses to the **Sierra Nevada** (50 mins). During the ski season, there are extra services leaving from a stand on Paseo del Violón.

Other Andalucían destinations include: **Sevilla** (8 daily, 3 hrs), **Jaén** (more than hourly, 1 hr) and **Málaga** (hourly, 2 hrs), **Córdoba** (8 daily, 2 hrs 30 mins), **Almería** (7 daily, 2 hrs 15 mins), and **Cazorla** (2 daily, 4 hrs).

Long distance Major destinations outside Andalucía include **Valencia** (6 daily; 7 hrs 30 mins to 9 hrs), **Madrid** (10 daily, 5 hrs), and **Barcelona** (5 daily, 13 hrs).

Car

If arriving by car, the best option is to park it as soon as possible. Large tracts of the centre are only accessible to residents or those who are going to stay in the area. These zones are camera controlled; you can enter, but make sure your hotel registers your license plate number to the police, otherwise you'll get fined. If you've booked a hotel within the area blocked off by automated pillars, press the buzzer for your hotel on the console (if there is one), or give the operator the name of the hotel and your reservation number, and you'll be let through.

Parking Many hotels offer pricey parking; underground car parks will cost around €18-30 per day; the more expensive ones are nearest the old centre. Hotels without private parking usually have a discount arrangement with a car park; make sure you check this beforehand, as once you take the ticket from the machine, it may be too late.

Car hire At the airport: **Avis**, T958-446455, www.avis.com and **Europcar**, T958-245275, www.europcar.com, among others. These 2 are also at the train station.

Train

The train station is a 15-min walk west of the centre; a short walk brings you to Av de la Constitución from where the LAC bus will bring you to the centre.

In practice, there aren't many destinations for which this is a handier mode of transport than the bus, but **Ronda** (3 daily, 2 hrs 40 mins) is certainly one, and there are 4 daily trains to **Guadix** (1 hr) which are speedier than going by road. **Antequera** (8 daily, 1 hr 30 mins) is served regularly, as are **Sevilla** (4 daily, 3 hrs), **Algeciras** (3 daily, 4 hrs 30 mins) and **Almería** (4 daily, 2 hrs 15 mins). There are 2 direct fast trains to **Madrid** (4 hrs 30 mins) via **Córdoba** (2 hrs 30 mins) and a night train to **Barcelona** (11 hrs). Use the **Algeciras** lines if you want to reach **Córdoba** (by normal train) or **Málaga**, and change at **Bobadilla**.

Sierra
Nevada

★The Sierra Nevada, which translates into English more prosaically as Snowy Mountains, is the memorable backdrop to Granada's Alhambra: if you're lucky with the visibility, that is. Hardy climbers used to ascend the Camino de la Nieve (Route of the Snow) to bring back fresh ice for the Moorish rulers' cocktails, but now streams of cars with skis aboard make the journey up a smoothly contoured road.

The range boasts mainland Spain's highest peak and Europe's southernmost ski resort; out of season, the region offers excellent walking opportunities and a chance to bag a few summits without any Alpine training. The upper section is a national park, while the lower reaches are *parque natural*, with lesser degrees of protection. The bleak and rugged peaks are an incredible contrast to much of the scenery of Andalucía and deserve a visit, whatever the season.

Pradollano, whose name (which translates literally as 'flat meadow') gives no hint of its dramatic location at 2172 m on the slopes of the crooked witch-hat peak of Veleta. The bustling main resort of the Sierra Nevada is a well-equipped place to ski and is chock full of facilities and (while the snow's around) life. In summer it's still lively with walkers and day trippers, but off season it's a ghost town.

The road through town is one way, so you have to enter at the top of the hill and work your way down, or park in the huge multi-storey at the lower entrance to the settlement.

The ski season usually commences in December and lasts until April or later, although the high temperatures at this low latitude can sometimes disrupt this. Day passes cost a maximum of €47, or €280 for a flexible seven-day pass to be used at your leisure. There are over 100 runs, seven of them black. The ski-lift ascends to **Borreguiles**, where there's a dedicated snowboard slope, before heading up to the top of the runs.

Essential Sierra Nevada

When to go

If you're visiting during the ski season, you'll find that prices are sky-high; even unremarkable hotels charge well over €100 for a double. You're much better off pre-booking a package (including lift passes, ski hire and accommodation) online or via a travel agent. Arrive at the resort without having booked anything and you'll pay well over the odds, even if the hotels are half-empty.

Warning

The Sierra Nevada is a significantly high mountain zone. Although it may appear harmless in summer, mist and bad weather can descend at any time. The paths are well marked, so stick to them, and always be equipped for cold weather. On long day hikes, be prepared to stay overnight, just in case. Call 112 in all emergencies.

There are heaps of ski schools and equipment hire stores, and competition keeps the prices relatively low. Shop around before taking your pick. Prices for a day's hire of all the kit start at around €25, while a two-hour class for two costs around €40-50. A recommended school, who also do snowboard lessons, kids' classes and equipment hire, is the **Escuela Oficial de Esquí** ① *Edif Telecabina, T958-480011, www.sierranevadaescuela.com.*

Walking

For all walks, make sure you are equipped with a decent map. The free sheets from the tourist offices won't do, even for the shortest stroll, so invest a few euros in a 1:25,000 scale map of the area.

Above Pradollano is Veleta, the second highest peak in the Spanish peninsula. A road from the resort leads a further 3 km uphill to Hoya de la Mora, where there are car parks, cafés and a tourist kiosk. It's about three hours to the summit of Veleta (3394 m) from here; it's an easy enough hike in late spring and summer (although take warm clothing), but ask for advice from October onwards. In summer, a bus runs 5 km past Hoya de la Mora a few times a day, cutting an hour off the climb. The road, which continues across the sierra to Capileira in the Alpujarra, is now closed to normal traffic year round. The walk to Capileira from the car park is at least eight to 10 hours but spectacular on both the ascent and descent.

From Hoya de la Mora, you can conquer mainland Spain's two highest mountains, Veleta and Mulhacén, in one go, although you'll have to be prepared to stay in the mountains overnight. Ascend to Veleta and, descending a short way, cut right along the ridge; Mulhacén (3479 m) is about another three hours from here. On the way back, there are two unmanned *refugios* you can make use of, **La Caldera**, on the way down to Capileira, or **La Carihuela**, near the summit of Veleta.

Less challenging hikes run from the car park downhill along ridges towards the information office. The office itself can provide details of these. See La Alpujarra, page 49, for more walking options to the Sierra Nevada peaks. For more detail, **Cicerone** ⓘ *www.cicerone.co.uk*, publish a good walking guide to the Sierra Nevada.

Listings Pradollano

Tourist information

El Dornajo information centre
On the main road 8 km before the ski resort, T958-340625. Daily 0930-1430, 1630-1930.
The centre has maps and walking advice and can book walking, riding and hang-gliding in spring and summer. For skiing conditions, see www.sierranevadaski.es or T902-708090. For information on accommodation contact the tourist offices in Granada.

Where to stay

There are numerous apartments for rent in the resort; see www.turgranada.es for a list. There are a few *hostales*, hotels and restaurants strung along the highway, but most of the accommodation and eating options are in Pradollano itself.

€€€€ Vincci Rumaykiyya
T958-482508, www.vinccihoteles.com. Nov-Apr.
More or less the most luxurious of the resort's options, this is right by a chairlift stop at the top of the settlement. 5-star facilities include pool and spa complex for ironing out the post-slope creases and a creche to look after the younger generation. You can get some excellent deals (€€) booking in advance via their website.

€€€ Trevenque
Plaza de Andalucía s/n, T958-465022, www.apartahoteltrevenque.com.
This hotel is one of the resort's better designed, in an attractive vine-covered stone building looking over the valley. Most of the rooms are apartment style – book ahead for the best rates – and there's a comfortable lounge with a view.

€ Albergue Sierra Nevada
C Peñones 22, Pradollano, T955-035886, www.inturjoven.com. Open all year.

Right at the top of town, this spacious modernized official youth hostel has a great position and snowy vistas. There are 4-bed dorms and a few doubles. There are also 6 self-contained apartments sleeping 4.

Restaurants

€€€ Ruta del Veleta
Edificio Bulgaria s/n, T958-486134, www.rutadelveleta.com. Nov-Apr.
The resort's best restaurant should be reserved ahead as its cosy rustic dining room, ceiling festooned with ceramic jugs, is popular after a day on the slopes. Dishes combine local ingredients with a gourmet, French-influenced touch, but the tradition of 30 years of mountain hospitality means there's no over-elaboration.

What to do

Gran Aventour, *C Cerro del Oro 20, Granada, T958-091662, www. granaventour.com.* Apart from ski schools in the resort, this outfit organizes various activities in the Sierra Nevada area, including canyoning, walking, rafting and cross-country skiing.

Transport

Bus
There are 3 daily buses to the Sierra Nevada (50 mins) from Granada. During the ski season, there are extra services (up to 4 a day, depending on conditions) leaving from a stand on Paseo del Violón. In season, there are also special services from Madrid via Granada.

Car
The main road winds 35 km southeast from Granada up to the main ski resort. The easiest way up from Granada by car is to head along C Acera del Darro, cross the bridge and follow the signs straight on up. The road is well ploughed in winter, but there are places to hire snow chains on the way up.

If your car is in reasonable shape and you don't mind steep and narrow roads, there's a spectacular and little-used climb that's not much more than an asphalted footpath (also a great walk). Exit the A395 8 km from Granada and follow the signs for Güejar-Sierra (for those on foot, regular buses run to this town from Granada). From Güejar, follow C Maitena out of town, eventually passing the restaurant of the same name, and follow signs to **El Charcón** restaurant. Keep going, and you'll climb sharply through walnut and chestnut trees, finally emerging above the Sierra Nevada information bureau (turn right to reach it and the main road to Pradollano, turn left for the more picturesque route to the ski resort). If you'd prefer to use this route on the way down (good brakes essential), turn off the main road at the information centre and take a left down the lane signposted to the Seminario. Either way, it's an unforgettable journey, but not to be attempted in icy conditions.

On foot
The road that crosses from the Alpujarra to the Sierra Nevada is closed to traffic, but walkable.

La Alpujarra

★La Alpujarra (or Las Alpujarras) is a fascinating and stunningly beautiful system of valleys and ravines isolated between two mountain ranges, the Sierra Nevada to the north, and the equally rugged Sierra de la Contraviesa to the south.

In Nasrid times, it was an important agricultural region, supplying Granada with vegetables and silk; after the fall of Granada, the Moors, upset with the ever-tightening strictures imposed on by the Catholic Monarchs, rose in two major revolts, both bloodily suppressed. The region then declined into rural poverty and, when the Guadix writer Pedro de Alarcón explored the region in the late 19th century, it was almost unknown.

In 1919, the Englishman Gerald Brenan (see box, page 63), walked in, pack on back and made his home at tiny Yegen. His post-war publication of his experiences, *South from Granada*, awakened foreign interest in the Alpujarra, which has been further put in the spotlight by more recent bestsellers *Driving over Lemons* and its sequels, written by ex-Genesis drummer Chris Stewart, who has made his home on a farm in the area.

While there are a lot of tourists, especially in summer, they come for two good reasons: the hiking through the valleys, hills, and mountains is some of Spain's best, and the villages and hamlets preserve some of the feel of the *morisco* culture that originally built them.

Puerto El Suspiro del Moro

Heading to the Alpujarra from Granada, the motorway crosses a low pass over the western foothills of the Sierra Nevada. The pass of the Moor's Last Sigh (Salman Rushdie named a novel after it), this is where Boabdil, last of the Nasrid rulers, turned back for a last look at the city over which the standards of Fernando and Isabel were now flying. His mother told him: "You weep as a woman for what you could not defend as a man." Thanks Mum!

Lanjarón

The first town in the Alpujarra, and one of the largest, Lanjarón's name might look familiar: that's because it adorns the labels of many Andalucían bottles of mineral water. The town gained fame in the early 20th century as a spa; the hillside is also riddled with fountains and springs (*fuentes* or *manantiales*), each of which claims to remedy a specific ailment.

Lanjarón has a different feel to the villages that draw visitors to the region; with its elegant avenue lined with plane trees, it could almost be in France. The spa is still very popular, particularly with people with rheumatic and arthritic complaints; there are various treatments available, from hydrotherapy and massages to mud showers.

At the entry to town, opposite the large spa hotel, is the **tourist office** ⓘ *T958-770462, Mon-Sat 1000-1400, 1630-2030 (1600-1900 winter), Sun 1000-1400*, which is good for specific information on walking routes around Lanjarón as well as maps and more general information on the Alpujarra.

There are several gentle walking trails north of town, as well as some more serious ascents of nearby hills and peaks. The tourist office has a couple of map sheets. You can also join the GR-7 path here and work your way up to the villages of the High Alpujarra. Pampaneira, via Cañar, is about six hours away.

Orgiva

Entering the Alpujarra proper, Orgiva (stress on the first syllable; *or*-hee-va) is the principal town of the western region, and sits in the middle of the valley cut by the river Guadalfeo. Although attractive enough, it's hardly a charming place, with a traffic-choked main street and profusion of expat residents. Nevertheless, it's handy as a service centre; there are a range of shops, a medical centre and a cinema (open weekends only). Just after crossing the bridge to enter town, **tourist information** ⓘ *C Fuente Mariano 1, T958-784484, www.turismoalpujarra.com, Mon-Fri 0900-1400, 1700-1900, Sat 1000-1400*, is tucked away behind the petrol station. They are helpful and can book you accommodation in the whole region.

Orgiva's main monument is its church, with twin pointed towers. Inside, under a florid late Baroque dome and cupola, the ornate gilt pulpit stands out in front of a *retablo* with a recessed Crucifixion. The remains of a Moorish watchtower are nearby.

Essential La Alpujarra

Getting around

The Alpujarra region runs due east from Lanjarón. The western zone is the most picturesque but also the most touristy. From Orgiva, a road runs along the northern edge of the Alpujarra, winding through some of the most attractive villages that cling to the southern slopes of the Sierra Nevada. The quicker southern route heads east into the heart of the area towards the chief town of the eastern zone, Ugíjar. These parts are more barren and isolated. Another route could take you through the less-visited Sierra de la Contraviesa, further to the south.

There are petrol stations just past Pampaneira and between Pitres and Pórtugos, and then not until Cádiar.

La Alpujarra has many bus services between the main centres, with less frequent ones linking smaller settlements.

See also Transport, pages 53, 60, 62 and 65.

When to go

If you're planning to do some walking, by far the best times are spring, with a riot of wildflowers, and autumn, when temperatures have cooled and villagers are busy picking grapes, peppers and chestnuts. If you plan on walking into the Sierra Nevada, perhaps ascending mainland Spain's highest peak, Mulhacén, be aware that this is a much more serious exercise after September, when the temperature drops sharply at the higher altitudes. Walking in summer is a possibility, but take it easy: the sun is fierce, particularly at altitude. Be warned that during Easter, summer and other major European holiday times, the Alpujarra gets very crowded with visitors.

Tourist information

Tourist offices in Granada, Lanjarón and Orgiva can provide information on the Alpujarra. It's worth stocking up on maps and information in these places as in the smaller villages further into the region, information is sparser. In some places, private tour companies can help visitors with impartial advice. There are also information offices and kiosks in other villages.

Listings Western Alpujarra

Where to stay

Lanjarón

€€ Hotel El Sol
Av de la Alpujarra 30, T958-770130, www.hotelelsol.es.
While most visitors understandably push on through Lanjarón to other villages, this is a fine all-round option. The good-value rooms are clean and comfortable, equipped with heating, phone and TV, and there's a jacuzzi and sauna in the hotel. The café does excellent breakfast.

Orgiva

€€ Casa Rural Jazmín
C Ladera de la Ermita s/n, T958-784795, www.casaruraljazmin.com.

This French/Spanish-run guesthouse is at the top of the town, and a delightfully peaceful hideaway. The rooms are appealingly decorated in rustic style, and there's a garden with fruit trees and a pool. Prices include breakfast. The hosts are incredibly attentive and welcoming. Recommended.

€€ Hotel Taray Botánico
Ctra A-348 Km 18, T958-784525, www. hoteltaray.com.
A kilometre below town, this hotel sits in spacious grounds studded with palms and fruit trees. It boasts a big pool, Orgiva's best restaurant, and a row of well-equipped bungalow-style rooms with minibar; the more expensive of which have a private roof terrace (€€€). It's a very welcoming place.

Camping

Camping Orgiva
T958-784307, www.campingorgiva.com, 2 km below town near the river.
The better of the 2 campsites, this offers good facilities including pool and restaurant. It also has pretty and well-equipped bungalows (€€) sleeping 2-6, as well as a little cabin (€) on a platform for those with treehouse fantasies.

You can eat very well for very little in the Alpujarra. There are few gourmet choices, but nearly all the villages have at least a down-to-earth bar to try the delicious, no-frills Alpujarran cuisine, with dishes like local trout, *migas*, or the mixed platter *plato alpujarreño*, a meat-and-potatoes fix for the chilly nights. All to be washed down with simple but tasty *costa* wine.

Lanjarón

€€ Alcadima
C Tarrega 3, T958-770809, www. alcadima.com.
This romantic hotel restaurant offers great perspectives over the town and turns out very inventive neo-Moorish dishes in substantial portions. It's rapidly become one of the Alpujarra's best places to eat. Recommended.

Festivals

20 Jan **Feast of San Sebastián**, a big event in all Alpujarra villages.
Easter During **Semana Santa**, Orgiva celebrates a livestock fair that draws people from the whole region.
Late Sep Orgiva's fiestas.

What to do

See also page 134 for tour operators who run walking and other trips to the Alpujarra.
Agetrea, *www.andaluciaacaballo.org.* An association of various operators that run horse-riding trips in the Alpujarra and Sierra Nevada areas. Their website links to their pages where you can browse the trips.
Aventura Alpujarra, *T638-597715, www. aventuraalpujarra.es.* Based in Orgiva, organizes quad and mountain bike excursions as well as canyoning.
Aventura Polar, *T952-583945, www. puertodelaragua.com.* Based in winter at the *posada* on the road at the top of the Puerto de la Ragua pass, this set-up offers fun in the snow with activities like horse treks, husky sledging, and snowshoe walking.
Caballo Park, *T606-032005, www.caballopark.com.* 9 km from Orgiva on the Pampaneira road, is

Walking

This area is one of the country's most popular destinations for walking. There are numerous short-distance routes in and around the valleys, as well as the GR-7 long-distance path that crosses the region. Some paths are well waymarked, others less so or not at all.

For any walking in the region, it is essential to have a proper map. The most detailed maps available of the area are the 1:25,000 series of the Instituto Geográfico Nacional but these only cover small areas. It is perhaps best to stick with the Instituto Geográfico Nacional 1:50,000 map (*mapa* or *guía*) *Sierra Nevada*. Alpina's 1:40,000 map *Sierra Nevada/La Alpujarra* isn't bad although some tracks are missing from the map. The best place to pick up maps and guidebooks is in the Pampaneira visitor centre where the excellent Nevadensis guides are based (see What to do, below). Or buy Discovery Walking Guides *Las Alpujarras 1:40,000 Tour & Trail Map*, with detailed GPS information, before you go. You can purchase it from their website www.walking.demon.co.uk or download a digital edition.

Walking in the Alpujarra is mostly easy. Although there's a lot of up-and-down, the gradients aren't that steep and villages are closely spaced. The sun, however, even in spring and autumn, is intense, and you should be properly prepared for it. If walking above village level up towards the Sierra Nevada or similar, be prepared for bad weather at any time of year; if doing longer walks, be ready to stay a night at a *refugio*.

one of several that offer good excursions, from short treks (€35) to longer day or weekend escapes. Nevadensis, *Plaza de la Libertad, Pampaneira*, T958-763127, www. nevadensis.com. Highly recommended mountain and walking guides; also offer 4WD excursions, quad biking, and horse riding.

Transport

Bus

From Granada, **Lanjarón** is served by bus 6 to 9 times daily (1-1½ hrs depending on route). These buses continue to **Orgiva** (15 mins more). These buses are run by **Alsa**; timetables and tickets online at www.alsa.es.

High Alpujarra

La Alpujarra's most popular and delightful villages

Just before Orgiva, a road snakes off into the hills and along the northern edge of the Alpujarra; on this route are some of the region's best places, including Pampaneira, Bubión and Capileira, as well as the ham town of Trevélez.

Ascending above Orgiva, you soon pass a turn-off for Cañar, an untouristy place with fantastic views from its situation high above the central valley. There's a

Architecture, agriculture and crafts

The typical Alpujarran village consists of box-shaped houses traditionally roofed with a thick local clay called *launa*. They are closely packed together along narrow streets and up hillsides. All the villages today are whitewashed, but this is a recent innovation; Gerald Brenan (see box, page 63), on returning to Yegen in the 1950s, was surprised at the prosperity shown by the fact that several houses were now white.

The Alpujarran house is typically fairly large, with a storage/stable area on the ground floor and living quarters upstairs.

The Moors terraced and irrigated the Alpujarra, and their earthworks remain the basis of the region's agriculture. Watercourses (*acequías*) are still of paramount importance; each farm along an *acequía*'s route has rights to divert the waterflow for a couple of hours; this is done with guillotine-like metal slabs. The region is astonishingly fertile, and produces almost every sort of Mediterranean vegetable; staples are grapes, peppers, potatoes, almonds, onions and chestnuts.

The Alpujarra was once famous for its silks (see Brenan's *South from Granada*, for a hilarious description of the fussy silkworm's habits). These days there is a flourishing trade in *artesanía* (handcrafts), of which some are more traditional than others. Ceramics and leather are evident throughout, as well as thick woollen jerseys and socks. The New Age element in the valleys has added a different stylistic trend to the mixture.

whitewashed church and a central plaza with a fountain, but little going on. It's very unspoiled, and many houses still have the livestock living on the ground floor.

Locals are divided on the hippie community of **El Beneficio** that lies between here and Orgiva. A hardy year-round group lives there, bolstered by large numbers of part-time residents in spring and summer. The village, centred on a large and social tepee, runs along simple communal lines.

Pampaneira, Bubión and Capileira

These three villages are deservedly the most visited in the Alpujarra. Closely spaced, they perch on the Pampaneira gorge, a narrow offshoot from the central valley that is blessed with exceptionally fertile soil. All three have small supermarkets, ATMs and pharmacies, as well as a wide choice of eating and lodging options. There's a petrol station just beyond Pampaneira at the turn-off to the other two villages.

With the giant backdrop of the Sierra Nevada looming behind, it's no surprise to find that there's plenty of walking in the area. The Nevadensis office in Pampaneira or the park information office in Capileira can advise; also look out for the cheery walking pamphlets written by Elma Thompson, most of which leave from the villages in this zone.

The first village, Pampaneira, has a small main street and plaza; the rest of the village climbs up behind it. The whitewashed brick church is typical of the region, while the village's fountain dispenses virtue to those in need. **Nevadensis** ⓘ *Plaza Libertad s/n, T958-763127, www.nevadensis.com, Tue-Sat 1000-1400, 1600-1800 (1700-1900 summer), Sun and Mon 1000-1500*, is a helpful tour agency that gives regional information to visitors as well as offering guided walks in the Alpujarra and Sierra Nevada, horse trekking, canyoning and other activities.

A Tibetan monastery, **O Sel Ling** ⓘ *T958-343134, www.oseling.org,* is reached via a turn-off 5 km short of Pampaneira. The badly marked road is a poor one, deliberately so to discourage sightseeing, although interested visitors are welcome to visit part of the monastery. The site is impressive for its natural beauty and the decorative Buddhist elements. You can also arrange to stay on a retreat in simple accommodation or work as a volunteer.

Beyond Pampaneira, a turn-off leads further up the ravine to Bubión and Capileira. Both make good bases. Bubión's whitewashed church is below the main road in the Barrio Bajo; next door is the excellent **Casa Alpujarreña** ⓘ *Wed-Mon 1100-1400, Sat and Sun also 1700-1900, €2*, a museum in a large house that simply displays what a typical Alpujarran dwelling was like not so very long ago. The area only got running water in the 1970s, and many of the medieval farming implements on display are still in use. Note the collection of old newspapers with the Berlin airlift as one of the headlines: the house was acquired by the council from a deceased estate, and nothing had to be changed to convert it to a museum.

Capileira is the highest of the triumvirate, and a 30-minute walk beyond Bubión. Its higher altitude means it has more snow and wind than the lower villages. It is the best base for walking if you want to explore the high sierra, as a road (closed to traffic after a point) continues from here across the range to the Sierra Nevada ski resorts; from it climbs the main route to Spain's highest peak, Mulhacén. There's a helpful **peaks information office** ⓘ *T958-763090, www.magrama.gob.es, daily high summer 1000-1400, 1700-2000, otherwise Easter-early Dec Mon-Thu 1000-1400, Fri-Sun 1000-1400, 1600-1900*, on the main road. Ask them about weather conditions if you plan to walk further up into the mountains. There is a small **museum** ⓘ *C Mentidero, Tue-Sun 1130-1430, Sat also 1700-2000, €1*, about the writer Pedro de Alarcón, one of the first to make the Alpujarra known to a wider audience.

From Capileira, the road ascends a further 14 km up into the Sierra Nevada. A walkers' bus runs from Capileira up into the mountains daily from May to September, and at weekends only when conditions permit in autumn and winter. How far it goes depends on the snow, but in good conditions it climbs to Alto del Chorrillo, at 2700 m, from where it's only a four-hour return climb to the top of Mulhacén, or a seven-hour hike over the mountains and down to the Sierra Nevada ski resort of Solynieve. A useful *refugio* sits not far from Alto del Chorrillo, see Where to stay, below. From here you can also walk down to Trevélez in about 90 minutes, or walk back to Capileira. The information office has a leaflet detailing various suggested walks in conjunction with the bus service.

Mecina-Fondales and Ferreirola

Beyond the turn-off to Bubión and Capileira, the road continues towards Pitres. Halfway along, a small road leads down to the hamlets of Mecina-Fondales and Ferreirola. The latter has one of the region's most charming places to stay (see Where to stay, below).

Trevélez

This is the highest village in the Alpujarra (although the locals' claim that it's the highest in the country is false), with its highest part standing 1600 m above sea level. The altitude and clean mountain air are beneficial in the curing of hams, and the village's *jamón serrano* has traditionally been so good that the composer Rossini arranged for a constant supply of Trevélez ham to be sent to him.

These days, however, there are few pigs here, so the pig legs arrive in truckloads from elsewhere in Spain to be cured. The ham is still good and the industry employs most of the town's workforce. The main road is wall-to-wall shops selling *jamón* to people passing through, many of whom are anglers attracted by the river's fine trout.

Trevélez has three distinct barrios, a low, a medium and a high, separated by a good 150 m of altitude; it's a stiff climb to the top of the town from the main road.

Walking from Trevélez

Many people use Trevélez as a base for an ascent on Mulhacén, usually stopping at the Poqueira *refugio* en route (see Capileira, above, and Where to stay, below).

Another excellent walk is an all-day circuit from the village, one of the Alpujarra's most spectacular hikes. The distance covered is 14-15 km, and should take five to seven hours. There are some steep stretches, as you ascend to within 600 m of Mulhacén's summit. From Trevélez you have a climb of some 1200 m so to enjoy this walk you should be fairly fit and get going at a reasonable hour. You can shorten the walk by almost 6 km by ending the climb at the ruins of **Cortijo La Campiñuela**. In the colder months there is often snow on the higher sections of the walk so check before leaving Trevélez. The path followed on the circular option from La Campiñuela is steep and loose at times; if in doubt you can simply make this an up-and-down walk for as far as the mood takes you. **Map**: 1:50,000 Sierra Nevada General Map.

Juviles and Bérchules

Juviles is the next village along, after passing the intersection for Torvizcón (a good walk, see Torvizcón, page 60). Juviles is one of the region's most relaxed and welcoming villages, although there's not much in the way of sights.

Bérchules is, like everywhere, a town with good views, and this steep village has many houses prettily decorated with flowering pot plants and, in autumn, drying peppers.

Where to stay

Pampaneira, Bubión and Capileira

€€ Casa Belmonte
C Ermita s/n Bubión, T958-763135,
www.ridingandalucia.com.
Happiness in Bubión is a cute little
apartment with your own terrace to
marvel at the splendour of the view
down the valley. With a pretty twin
bedroom and a fold-out sofa, this is
exactly what is needed. The owner can
organize horse riding.

€€ Hotel Estrella de las Nieves
C de los Huertos s/n, Pampaneira, T958-
763981, www.estrelladelasnieves.com.
At the top of the village, this attractive
recent construction offers spectacular
views from its spacious a/c rooms.
There's a charming garden pool area
and both the staff and the breakfasts
are top-notch. Recommended.

€€ Hotel Real de Poqueira
C Doctor Castilla 11, Capileira, T958-
763902, www.hotelpoqueira.com.
This sturdy white building by the
church in Capileira is an excellent new
accommodation option. Very pleasing
modern rooms, a sweet pool and warm
hospitality make a home-from-home of
this enchanting village.

€ Hostal Pampaneira
C José Antonio 1, Pampaneira, T958-
763002, www.hostalpampaneira.com.
Spacious rooms with en suite bathroom;
the beds are decorated with *jarapa*
cloth. Breakfast is included. Downstairs
there's a bar and restaurant; the gruff
but good-natured boss has been dishing

out local food for years. It's good and
cheap, especially the fresh trout.

€ Las Terrazas de la Alpujarra
Placeta del Sol 12, Bubión, T958-763034,
www.terrazas alpujarra.com.
Excellent budget place, offering fine clean
rooms with bathroom complemented
by a cosy TV lounge, pool table, and
chirpy bird in a cage. There are also well-
equipped apartments and whole houses
for rent; these have kitchen, central
heating and fireplace. Recommended.

€ Refugio Poqueira
Between Capileira and Mulhacén, T958-
343349, www.refugiopoqueira.com.
Open all year.
Reserve accommodation and meals
ahead. At the foot of Mulhacén, this is
a large, simple but comfortable refuge
for walkers that serves warming meals.
Accommodation is in typical mountain-
hostel style, with mattresses side by side.
Shower and sheets are extra; meals cost
€17; they also do packed lunches.

Mecina-Fondales and Ferreirola

€€ Hotel Maravedí
C Fuente Escarda 5, Pitres, T958-766292,
www.hotelmaravedi.com.
Eco-friendly and run with a generous
personal touch, this is just the spot to
wind down for a couple of days. With
spacious, welcoming rooms, modern
and attractive bathrooms, and several
above-the-price-band facilities, it makes
a sound Alpujarra base.

€€ Sierra y Mar
Ferreirola, T958-766171, www.sierraymar.
com. Normally closed 1-2 months in
winter; check the website.

A top place to stay in this tiny village. Accommodation is in one of several self-contained rooms, many of which have a terrace, and all of which are individually decorated. Original Alpujarran furniture has been used as much as possible, and the low beds are designed for comfort. There's a lounge with books and a log fire, use of a kitchen, and a good breakfast included in the price, but the highlight is the genial hospitality of the owners, who are keen walkers. Highly recommended.

Trevélez

There's a wide choice of places to stay, with most of the options on the main road.

€€ Hotel La Fragua

C San Antonio 4, Barrio Medio, T958-858626, www.hotellafragua.com.
Simple and homely rooms in a pretty whitewashed building. Many have balconies. Worth the walk up the hill, but ring ahead, as it's often full with British walking groups. The more modern **Fragua 2** is behind the restaurant (worthwhile; see Restaurants) on the edge of the village and features sunnier, somewhat larger rooms with balconies.

€ Hostal Fernando

Pista del Barrio Medio s/n, T958-858565.
At the entrance to the middle section of town it enjoys a great setting with views, peace and quiet. The rooms are simple, but the balcony makes up for it. Private parking.

€ Pensión Mulhacén

T958-858587.
Run by a charming old couple, this *hostal* has 2 classes of room with a minimal difference in price, so go for the renovated ones, though the others are

perfectly serviceable. It's on the main road right at the bottom of things.

Camping

Camping Trevélez
1 km west of town, T958-858735, www.campingtrevelez.net.
Open all year (don't even think about pitching a tent in winter though).
A likeable campsite, one of the best in the Alpujarra. It's got a bar, pool, restaurant and play area for kids. There are several simple cabins sleeping 2 to 4, as well as tent and van sites.

Juviles and Bérchules

€€ Hotel Los Bérchules

Ctra Granada 20, Bérchules, T958-852530, www.hotel berchules.com.
This friendly modern hotel just below the village has well-equipped rooms with balconies, views, a pool and inviting lounge with a fireplace. It is great value, and the cheerful English-speaking owners can organize activities such as horse trekking and offer walking advice. There's a restaurant serving hearty Alpujarran fare; half-board is €21 per person.

€ El Paraje

Ctra Juviles–Bérchules, 500 m above the road between Juviles and Bérchules in the Parque Natural Sierra Nevada, T958-064029, www.elparaje.com.
This lovely spot is a large, traditional whitewashed farmhouse with 5 spacious, heated rooms that offer plenty of simple comfort. There are terrific views over the hills and valleys and acres of peace and quiet. They also have a compact self-catering apartment. Breakfast and other meals can be provided on request and you can rent mountain bikes to explore the area.

Restaurants

Pampaneira, Bubión and Capileira
See also Where to stay, above.
There are several eateries around
Pampaneira square.

€€ El Corral del Castaño
Plaza Calvario 16, Capileira, T958-763414.
This atmospheric rustic restaurant is on
the main plaza and makes an excellent
eating choice. There's a combination of
invention and tradition in the attractively
presented plates. Fine salads, tasty
grilled meats and a great pastry dish with
salmon and goat's cheese stand out.

€€ Estación 4
C Estación 4, Bubión, T651-831363.
Tue-Fri 1700-2300, Sat 1300-2300.
A winning combination of Mediterranean
food, teas and books drives business
at this inviting spot, well signposted
towards the bottom of the village. Tangy
tabbouleh, creamy hummus and seafood
spaghetti are among the draws.

€€ Teide
Ctra 2, Bubión, T958-763084, www.
restauranteteide.com.
On the main road, this is a redoubt
of traditional cooking, with typical
Alpujarran cuisine served up in the bar,
terrace, and an attractive dining room.
Trout with ham, *plato alpujarreño*, or
anything else is good. Recommended.

€ Bodega Alacena
Callejón de las Campanas s/n, Capileira,
T958-763268.
Tucked away down the side of the
church, this little gem sells delicious
chestnut honey, ham, wine and other
goodies, but also has a delightful
little bodega space where you can sit
down for wine and simple *raciones*.
Recommended.

Trevélez
As in much of the Alpujarra, many places
partially or fully close over winter.

€€ Mesón La Fragua
C Posadas s/n, along from the hotel
of the same name, T958-858573,
www.hotellafragua.com.
A cosy spot on the top floor with views
over the valley and very fair prices. Food
and service are to be admired here; the
ensalada de jamón (ham salad) is a meal
in itself, but leave room for the house
roast lamb, which is superb.

€€ Piedra Ventana
Ctra Ugíjar 36, T958-858599, www.
restaurantepiedraventana.com.
Near the bridge right at the bottom of
town, this has a traditional bar decorated
with cowbells and a dining area with
relaxing perspectives over the river.
They do a great line in local food.

€ Haraiçel
C Real s/n, T958-858530.
Unpretentious and notably welcoming
spot that isn't afraid to break Alpujarran
conventions on the menu. Pork loin in
raspberry sauce is one surprising but
tasty offering. For a real pig experience,
though, it has to be the *codillo*, a large
pork knuckle boiled to tenderness and
served with red cabbage and potatoes.
Wash it down with a jug of *costa* wine.

Festivals

20 Jan Feast of San Sebastián, a big
event in all Alpujarran villages.
13 Jun Trevélez's famous **Moors and
Christians fiesta**, with mock battles.
4-5 Aug *Romería* from Trevélez to
the top of Mulhacén via the Ermita
de San Antonio.
3rd weekend of Oct Trevélez's fiesta.

What to do

Tour operators
See page 52 and page 134 for tour operators who run walking and other trips to the Alpujarra.

See page 52 and page 134 for tour operators who run walking and other trips to the Alpujarra.

Transport

Bus
From Granada, there are buses 3 times daily to **Trevélez** (3 hrs 15 mins) via **Pampaneira**, **Bubión** and **Capileira** (2 hrs 25 mins). These buses are run by **Alsa**; timetables and tickets online at www.alsa.es.

Southern Alpujarra

superb views of wine-producing white villages and hamlets

From Orgiva, the A348 runs along the southern edge of the Alpujarra, linking up with the northern route again at Cádiar. Like in the song about Loch Lomond, the low road is faster than the high one, and, while not quite as dramatic, provides excellent and expansive views of the valley and the white villages on the other side.

Torvizcón and Cádiar
The only major village on the route is sleepy Torvizcón, prettily situated at the bottom of a *rambla* (stony gully). It's got a bulky church and a ruined Moorish tower, and there's a small *esparto* **museum** at the far end of town. *Esparto* is the sturdy grass traditionally used in Andalucía to make baskets, blinds, mats and wall-hangings.

From just beyond Torvizcón, a narrow road cuts across the valley and up the other side towards Trevélez, passing the tiny hamlet of Almegíjar en route. It's a stunning drive and best done in this direction for your brakes' sake. Walking, it's less arduous to come the other way. Follow the road down from the junction between Trevélez and Juviles, bearing right as soon as you reach the deserted mining village.

The village of **Cádiar**'s central position and the fact that it is the hub of the region's road system mean that at some point you'll likely fetch up here. It's not particularly pretty, but it's a sociable place, particularly at the beginning of October, during its fiesta, when the best of the Alpujurran village fountains, the Fuente del Vino, is set up for a week in the main square dispensing *costa* wine to all comers. The town's name derives from the Arabic word *qadi*, meaning judge; this was probably where the local one resided.

Ugíjar more or less marks the eastern end of the Granadan part of the Alpujarra, but beyond it are more delights in its eastern, Almerían portion. It's a busy but not unattractive one-street service town with a couple of cheap lodging options, a tourist office, petrol station and places to eat.

Sierra de la Contraviesa

From the Orgiva–Torvizcón road, you could strike off on another circuit through the southern Sierra de la Contraviesa to Albuñol via several less touristy villages, and then to Cádiar or, indeed, down to the coast a few kilometres away.

From the turn-off some 6 km from Orgiva, the road (signposted Albuñol) ascends a craggy valley to a pass, where magnificent views over the sierra, coast, and sea suddenly open up. From here, the road winds its way eastwards to Albuñol, passing several picturesque wine-growing *pueblos* en route; it's worth making a detour to investigate them, as they are traditional and mostly unspoiled by tourism. There's little in the way of gourmet restaurants, but every village has its little bar where you can try a glass of the local *costa* wine and munch on bread and ham.

Albuñol is a large, sprawling town that has very little appeal and nowhere to stay. It does, however, have the **Cueva de los Murciélagos**, which produced some remarkable neolithic basketwork on display in Granada's archaeological museum (see page 23).

From Albuñol, you can head south to the coast road 7 km away, or head north to **Albondón**, a pleasant wine-producing village, and on to **Cádiar**, the hub of the Alpujarra proper, or to Ugíjar, via the picturesque town of Murtas, another wine centre. The distinctive muddy-coloured *costa* wine here is popular in the Alpujarra region and should be tried at least once; cheaper examples are much better with food than on their own.

Listings Southern Alpujarra

Where to stay

Torvizcón and Cádiar

€€ **Alquería de Morayma**
Ctra A348, Km 52, 3 km from Cádiar, down the Torvizcón road, T958-343221, www.alqueriamorayma.com.
This is an utterly rustic and peaceful hideaway, surrounded by an ecologically minded farm producing wine and olive oil. There's a variety of rooms designed in traditional Alpujarran style. From apartments equipped with fridge and stove to a room in a whitewashed chapel, all have clay tiled floors, Moorish tracery and prints, ceilings with wooden beams and iron bedheads. There's a pool and a restaurant.

Restaurants

Torvizcón and Cádiar
See also Where to stay, above.

€ **Parada Bar**
Plaza España 12, Cádiar.
Local in character, this bar on the square is coloured a rather garish orange but is an atmospheric spot for a tapa, with its conversations about the grape harvest and noticeboard with donkeys and tractors for sale.

Festivals

20 Jan Feast of San Sebastián, a big event in all Alpujarran villages.
Early Oct Cádiar's knees-up with its fountain of wine.

2nd week of Oct Ugíjar has some well-attended fiestas, revolving around livestock and drinking.

What to do

Tour operators
See page 52 and page 134 for tour operators who run walking and other trips to the Alpujarra.

See page 52 and page 134

Transport

Bus
There are 2 daily buses from Granada to **Ugíjar** (4½ hrs) via Torvizcón and Cádiar. Buses to **Almería** via **Berja** leave 2-3 times daily from the centre of Ugíjar, and a couple of daily buses run to Laroles from Ugíjar.

There's a daily bus from Granada to **Albuñol** (3½ hrs), via Orgiva and the road junctions for villages on this route.

Northeastern Alpujarra

Gerald Brenan's house and spectacular mountain walks

From Cádiar or Bérchules, you can follow the twisty road along the northern edge of the Alpujarra, more interesting than the road that heads due east via Yátor to Ugíjar. The first village is Mecina Bombarón, with several *casas rurales* and a hotel.

Yegen, Válor and Mairena
Described in detail in *South from Granada* by Gerald Brenan (see box, opposite), the village where the author lived is still very typical of the Alpujarra, if you discount the central fountain, which Brenan would be highly amused to see is now a replica of that in the Court of Lions in the Alhambra. Just below this square is Brenan's old house, No 28, marked by a small plaque. If you've seen the film of the book, you'll recognize the village.

Válor, the next town to Yegen, is one of the little-visited gems of the Alpujarra. Still very much reliant on local industry rather than tourism, you can visit the small factories that produce olive oil, cheese and soap or just enjoy wandering around the streets. The whitewashed church has a brick bell tower but an unadorned interior. There's a bank, ATM, pharmacy, and good accommodation and eating.

From Válor, a 15-minute climb will take you to the hamlet of **Nechite**, a tiny place with excellent views from the terrace beside its church. Beyond Válor, you pass through **Mecina Alfahar**, a shady vine-laced village, and arrive at pretty **Mairena**, with views over its plentiful olive groves. From Mairena, you can ascend to lovely **Júbor**, a tiny village reached in 10 minutes on foot through a chestnut grove. There's a red-roofed church as well as a small bar serving food, and a view over the spiny rock ridges below.

Laroles
This seldom-visited town marks the end of the northern route along the Alpujarra; from here you can descend to Ugíjar via Cherín or climb over the Sierra Nevada

ON THE ROAD
Don Gerardo

On the wall of a house, just off a small square in the Alpujarran village of Yegen, is a tiny plaque that proclaims in blue letters that the English writer Gerald Brenan lived here in the 1920s and 1930s. This is a modest tribute to someone whom many consider to be the greatest British Hispanist.

Brenan was born in Malta in 1894 and after a public school education, he fought in the First World War, gaining a Military Medal and the French Croix de Guerre. He became acquainted with the Bloomsbury Group after the war, but soon tired of what he saw as the sexual hypocrisies of British life, and headed for Spain, drawn as much as anything by the cheap wine and cigarettes, his lifelong addictions. He lived in the then remote village of Yegen, with his collection of over 2000 books. Don Gerardo, as locals knew him, intimately describes the village in *South from Granada*, regarded as a sociological masterpiece and now made into a film.

In Yegen he had a steamy relationship with a 15-year-old local girl, Juliana, resulting in a daughter, Elena. In 1930, Brenan, back temporarily in England, met the American poet Gamel Woolsey, whom he married; the couple returned to Spain. Brenan took his daughter from Juliana and renamed her Miranda Helen; he only saw Juliana once more, reintroducing her to her own daughter on the condition that she didn't reveal who she was.

Brenan published several other books about Spain and its people. He developed a strong Andalucían dialect and a love for the Spanish, a two-way rapport as his passionate writing found an appreciative readership in Spain.

Brenan was also an assiduous correspondent and wrote at length to contemporaries in Britain, especially the Bloomsbury circle. Indeed, his biographer, Jonathon Gathorne-Hardy, believes that his brilliant letters will "eventually prove Gerald's most lasting memorial". Gerald Brenan moved to England at the outbreak of the Civil War until 1949, when he settled in Churriana near Málaga. *The Face of Spain* was a personal account of this time. In his later years, Brenan enthusiastically embraced the hippy culture of Torremolinos, despite being in his late sixties. After the death of his wife, he moved in with a much younger woman in the village of Alhaurín el Grande. Finally, at the age of 90, he returned to England, staying in an old people s home in Pinner. Brenan was always more highly regarded in Spain than in England and the Spanish press spread the idea that he had returned to England against his will. Eventually a delegation from Alhaurín came to Pinner and virtually kidnapped Brenan and returned him to Andalucía. He was installed in a home in Alhaurín, the Regional Government providing a nurse and covering his living expenses until he died in 1987. He left his body to medical science but no-one at Málaga university wanted to take a scalpel to such a significant figure, so he was finally buried next to his wife in Málaga's English cemetery in 2001.

north to Guadix (see page 67). The road that reaches Laroles from Mairena is spectacular, in some places offering almost a 360-degree panorama of the valleys below. Laroles makes a good base for the Eastern Alpujarra with its views, accommodation and sociable folk. There's also a small **tourist office** ① *Fri 1700-2100 (1900 winter), Sat-Sun 1000-1400.*

There are several **walking trails** around Laroles, including the one that climbs to the pass of La Ragua (see below), which is a full day's ascent. A fascinating shorter walk of two to three hours runs in a loop up the valley of the Río Laroles, following the main Moorish aqueduct of the region, the Acequia Real. Walk back along the main road towards Mairena and turn right shortly after crossing the Río Laroles, just before the road crosses a gravelly gully, the **Barranco del Arena**. The path climbs along the gully, then cuts right, following the Laroles valley. The *acequia* comes in on your left; at the point where it meets the river a couple of kilometres upstream, cross the small bridge and bear right, following the valley back down to Laroles down what was once the old muleteers' path over the Sierra Nevada. The tourist office has maps of this and other walks, as do the campsites.

Puerto de la Ragua

From Laroles you can ascend to Puerto de la Ragua, a 2000 m-high pass over the Sierra Nevada. It's a memorable drive through increasingly bleak mountain scenery. At the top, where there's a small ski resort, you begin a steep descent to the sheet-like plains east of Guadix, dominated by the highly memorable castle of La Calahorra (see page 69).

You can also climb a forested path from Laroles; this takes six to seven hours, so book a bed up the top and be prepared for poor weather, particularly in spring and autumn. The trail ascends through a fertile corner before climbing through pine forest. The total distance is 18 km, and is of medium difficulty. From the top, the GR-7 trail continues down to La Calahorra, and if you have time, you should walk this leg too; a stunning descent down to the plains. At the pass is a year-round *refugio* (see Where to stay, below).

Listings Northeastern Alpujarra

Where to stay

Yegen, Válor and Mairena

€€ Las Chimeneas
C Amargura 6, Mairena, T958-760089, www.alpujarra-tours.com.
A charming *casa rural* easily accessed at the bottom of this village, this offers valley views and spacious rooms with balcony. There are also self-catering houses

and apartments in adjacent buildings. Breakfast is included, other meals are available, and they can do anything from setting you off on a self-guided walk to arranging a week-long extravaganza of guided outdoors and cultural activities.

€ La Fuente
C Real 46, Yegen, T958-851067.
This great-value cheapie in Yegen offers simplicity but authenticity, 3 spotless

cool rooms, and a location right on the square. The attractive *comedor* also does local dishes.

Laroles
See **Balcón de la Alpujarra** in Restaurants, below.

Apartments

€€ Hotel Real de Laroles
C Real 46, T958-760058, www. turismoruralaroles.com.
Near the plaza at the base of the village, this is one of the region's more charming options, a delightfully homely family-run place decorated in simple but appealing rural style with wrought-iron bedsteads and cut-glass lampshades. There are roof spaces with awesome views and the welcome is generous, as is the delicious mountain fare in the adjacent restaurant.

Puerto de la Ragua

€ Albergue Puerto de la Ragua
T950-524020, www.puertodela ragua.com. Open year round.
Right at the top of the pass, this *refugio* is a popular base for cross-country skiing in winter and walkers in summer, and has 32 dorm beds, and a restaurant serving lunches and dinners.

Restaurants

Laroles
As well as the restaurant at the Hotel Real, the **€ Balcón de la Alpujarra**, T958-760217, appeals as a place to eat for its cheap local dishes and inexpensive *menú del día*, but most of all its top views over the valley below. They also have rooms (**€**), some with kitchen.

Festivals

20 Jan Feast of San Sebastián, a big event in all Alpujarran villages.
Mid-Sep In Válor you can see another of the region's best **Moros y Cristianos** festivals.

What to do

See page 52 and page 134 for tour operators who run walking and other trips to the Alpujarra.

Transport

Bus
There are 2 daily buses from **Granada** to Yegen, and Válor. A couple of daily buses run to Laroles from **Ugíjar**.

East from
Granada

Heading east from Granada into the long 'handle' of the province, the landscape becomes increasingly rugged. At its extremity, it's one of the most rewarding remote regions of Andalucía.

Many of the towns and villages in this area have substantial barrios where people live in caves, which were traditionally a cheap place to live and a way of avoiding temperature extremes. One such town is Guadix, which also has a striking cathedral.

Near here, the extraordinary castle at La Calahorra is a must-see, while the little known valley of Gorafe has hundreds of well-excavated prehistoric tombs to investigate.

From the town of Baza, surrounded by *parque natural*, you can head northwards towards the Sierra de Cazorla through some impressive jagged terrain, or up towards the remote sheep-rearing town of Huéscar and on towards Almería province or Murcia.

★Arriving for the first time, the town of Guadix seems as if it's an offworld colony, set among otherworldly crags sharply eroded into fey formations. When the wind blows through here in winter, you can feel why the rocks have crumbled before it. Troglodyte communities are important parts of Guadix and most of the towns and villages in this area. Guadix also has a stunning cathedral and array of other monuments, but the rest of the town is impoverished, with few employment prospects and tension between its gypsy and *payo* communities.

Guadix's helpful **tourist office** ⓘ *Pl de la Constitución 15, T958-662804, www.guadix.es, Mon-Fri 0900-1400, 1600-1800*, is in the old town near the cathedral.

The centre of Guadix is dominated by its memorable **cathedral** ⓘ *T958-665108, Mon-Sat 1040-1400, 1600-1800, 1700-1930 summer, €5*, built from a dusky orange sandstone and overlooking the bare space that was once Guadix's prosperous Jewish quarter. It was built in different periods: the Isabelline Gothic interior has a Renaissance apse by Diego de Siloé, and there are two exuberantly Baroque façades on the exterior. The brick bell tower adds another ingredient to the mix, but when the sun shines, it's one of the more remarkable buildings in Andalucía. The main façade is pure Spanish Baroque, full of niches and columns. Move to your right to where a street cuts in behind you and observe how the façade suddenly realigns itself with the white saints all in a line.

The interior is gloomy by comparison; the highlight is the very ornately carved choir stalls. The Guadix choirboys have achieved some fame in Spain and sold many albums. Note the contrast between the earlier Gothic part and the simpler Renaissance classicism with its round arches and smooth lines. The museum (included in the admission) is disappointing; among some worthwhile religious art is a surfeit of showy silver and hoarded 'treasures'.

Opposite the cathedral, you can head under an arch into the charming **Plaza Constitución**. In this old part of town are also a couple of fine Renaissance palaces, the **Palacio de Peñaflor** by the Alcazaba, and the **Palacio de Villalegre** behind the cathedral. Both built in the 16th century, they are similarly designed, with twin brick towers flanking a façade decorated with coats of arms. Below the Palacio de Peñaflor, the **Iglesia de Santiago** has an excellent *mudéjar* wooden ceiling. Guadix's most famous citizen, the writer Pedro Antonio de Alarcón, is commemorated with a small statue in the *alameda* below the cathedral.

Guadix's once-proud Moorish **Alcazaba** now has its walls bolstered by decaying concrete. Built in the 10th century, it offers little more than wistful historical reminders of Guadix's more prosperous days and is currently closed to the public. As well as the Alcazaba, significant stretches of Moorish walls still encircle the old town.

Though most spaghetti western filming in Spain took place around Almería, Guadix had its moment in the limelight too – it featured as the Mexican town of Mesa Verde in Sergio Leone's *A Fistful of Dynamite*.

However, Guadix's biggest silver screen celebrity is 'Baldwin', a glorious old 1928 steam train sitting with its four carriages in a shed near the station. It has starred in dozens of films, including *Dr Zhivago*, *The Good, the Bad and the Ugly*, and *Indiana Jones and the Last Crusade*. Despite not being officially open to the public – though plans are afoot – ask around the station, for it is lovingly maintained by train buffs who are delighted to show it off.

The caves

There are several consecutive cave suburbs encircling the town's southern edges. They are bizarrely picturesque, with chimneys emerging from the hillside like comedy toadstools alongside radio aerials hung with washing. It's pleasant to wander around the area, but avoid rubbernecking. You may be lured into 'tours' of private homes; these are best avoided, as nasty scenes can ensue when an exorbitant sum is demanded on your exit.

A couple of caves are open to the public. The **Centro de Interpretación Cuevas de Guadix** ⓘ *Pl Padre Oveda s/n, T958-665569, www.cuevamuseoguadix.com, Mon-Fri 1000-1400, 1600-1800 (1700-1900 summer), Sat 1000-1400, €2.60*, has an interesting display on troglodyte life.

Guadix has several accommodation options in caves, and there are dozens more in surrounding towns and villages; contact the tourist office for details.

Listings Guadix

Where to stay

The main reason to stay in Guadix is to experience one of its several cave hotels, which are rather more luxurious than they may sound. As well as those mentioned here, the tourist office can provide a list of further troglodyte options.

€€ Cuevas de Rolando
Rambla de Baza s/n, 3 km from the centre of Guadix, T670-799138, www.cuevasderolando.com.
These are some of the most atmospheric caves available, with uplifting views to be enjoyed from your little private patio at the cave mouth. Inside, they are decorated with style and charm by the friendly owners.

€€ Cuevas El Abuelo Ventura
Ctra de Lugros s/n, about 1 km out of Guadix T958-664050, www.cuevas abueloventura.com.
This is a fairly luxurious trog option, though the fact that the caves aren't natural might put you off. Spacious, comfortable dens have good facilities and views from the front; there's a restaurant and even a pool half-in and half-out of a cave. It needed a facelift at our last visit.

Restaurants

€€ Boabdil
C Manuel de Falla 3, T958-664883, www.restauranteboabdilguadix.com.
This is one of Guadix's better eateries. Apart from the usual hearty meat dishes, there's some excellent grilled fish, and

a thoughtful selection of mid-priced Spanish wines. Among the starters, the unusual pineapple and asparagus salad has plenty going for it, as does the smoked salmon.

Transport

Bus

Buses run roughly hourly to **Granada** from Guadix's bus station, by the river to the east of town (1 hr), and to **Almería** almost as often (1 hr 20 mins). Trains run the same route 4 times daily (1 hr), or the other way to Almería. Other bus services run regularly to the surrounding villages, including **La Calahorra**. **Madrid** is served 5 times daily (5 hrs), while on Mon, Wed, Fri, a bus heads to Almería over the **Puerta de la Ragua**. **Baza** is served hourly.

La Calahorra

a compulsory stop for the amazing castle

★The town of La Calahorra is famous for its stunning castle which wholly dominates the surrounding countryside. To call this one of the most dramatic and unexpected castles in Spain is no exaggeration. Although from the outside it may look every inch a purely functional fortification, it is in fact more of a palace than a redoubt.

To visit the **castle** ⓘ *Wed only, 1000-1300, 1600-1800, entrance by gratuity*, outside of the opening times call on the keyholder, Antonio, at Calle Claveles 2, T958-677098, just down from Labella *hostal*. He'll usually be happy to take you up, but he's only doing you a favour, so don't complain if he's got something better to do, and do tip generously if he does. Remember that 1400-1700 are sacred lunch and siesta hours.

The exterior conceals one of the earliest Renaissance interiors in Spain, created on the whim of Rodrigo de Vivar y Mendoza, an illegitimate son of a duke whose life reads like a cheap historical novel. Fleeing persecution by the aristocracy after the death of his father and first wife, he headed to Italy, where he fell under the spell of the pope's daughter, Lucrezia Borgia. He returned to Spain without an Italian consort but with a head full of the new architectural ideas of that region. The palace was a result of that, but no sooner was it completed than Rodrigo was forced to leave the area; old-seated prejudices compounded by the marquis's scandalous private life made residence in Granada province a very hot potato. It's now owned by another ducal family, who are suspicious of the state's attempts to open it to tourism.

The road to the top is a poor one, so if it's your own beloved car you may want to spare it the climb; in any case, the walk to the top heightens the anticipation, as the unlikely building looms menacingly above.

From La Calahorra you can ascend the GR-7 path up to Puerto de la Ragua (see page 64) and down again into the Alpujarra. The ascent to the pass takes some six to eight hours, with spectacular views all the way, and you can stay in the *refugio* up the top (see Where to stay, page 65).

Where to stay

€€ El Castillo/Hospederia del Zenete
Ctra La Ragua s/n, T958-677192, www.
hospederiadelzenete.com.
This well-appointed hotel is somewhat
tastelessly built to resemble the castle
itself, but has a range of comfortable
accommodation, ranging from attractive
standard doubles to split-level suites and
a family apartment. There's also a gym
and sauna. The restaurant is the best in

town, and serves generous portions of
heartily flavoured local fare. Service is lax
but willing.

€ Hostal Labella
Ctra de Aldeire 1, T958-677241.
A modern choice offering excellent
value, rooms have heating, bathroom,
phone and TV. Most importantly, half of
them have a balcony that looks directly
at the magnificent castle. Downstairs is a
convivial bar and restaurant.

Gorafe
remarkable place with late-Neolithic tombs, hidden deep in Granada province

★Gorafe is almost never visited except by *granadinos*, but that will surely
change. Crossing a flat arid plain punctuated with olive trees, the ground
suddenly gives way and a picturesque canyon opens up. Apart from the walking
and photographic opportunities, there are some 200 painstakingly excavated
and labelled late-Neolithic tombs in the immediate vicinity to investigate.

You can pick up a map of the tombs at the Gorafe town hall or from the **Centro de
Interpretación Sobre El Megalítico** ① *A92, T958-693159, www.gorafe.es, Tue-Sun
1100-1600, €3*, on the motorway 20 km from Guadix towards Murcia. This unusual
underground museum is set up to resemble a dolmen burial chamber and brings
the tombs to life with information and a flashy 3D audiovisual.

The village of Gorafe itself has plenty of unspoilt charm, including many
cave dwellings around its edges. Several of the caves have been converted to
comfortable apartments in which you can stay (if travelling by public transport
you'll have to). These can get busy with *granadino* families at weekends, so it's
better to book ahead.

To get there by car, take the Baza–Murcia road from Guadix and exit the
autopista 16 km from town; Gorafe is signposted, and is 13 km to the north of the
junction. If returning to Guadix or Granada by car, it's worth continuing up the
road to Alicún and Villanueva, then descending via the NE51 to Pedro Martínez;
the drive is spectacular.

Where to stay

€€-€ **Las Cuevas del Pataseca**
C La Mina 43, T958-693114.
Ignacio has beautifully done up, colourful cave apartments at reasonable prices.

Transport

Bus
A daily bus leaves **Guadix** for Gorafe at 1430. The return bus leaves at 0730.

Baza

historic town making a decent stopover

Heading northeast from Guadix the scenery becomes increasingly rugged, and the olive tree increasingly predominant. The road passes through the Parque Natural Sierra de Baza before dramatically descending to the town of Baza, which has a much more peaceful and friendly feel than Guadix.

Baza was once an important Iberian town known as Basti, and it was here that one of the finest pre-Roman pieces unearthed by archaeologists in Spain was found: the *Dama de Baza*, an enigmatic roughly life-size sculpture of a woman of such beauty and importance that it was quickly whisked away to Madrid, where it can be seen in the city's archaeological museum. The Moors held on to Baza until 1489, when Castilian armies finally took its hill fortress. From that period the town has been a peaceful rural backwater and service town for the surrounding agricultural area.

Baza has been wracked by earthquakes over the years, which have damaged and destroyed many of its historic buildings. The old quarter is centred around Plaza Mayor, whose pleasing fountain is surrounded by roses. On this square are two of the most important edifices: the Colegiata, a high fortress-like church adorned with a Plateresque and a Baroque portal and some fine coats of arms. It is much revered for being the resting place of the local patron, San Máximo. Part of it was designed by the budding architect Alonso de Covarrubias, who was to rise to become one of the stars of the Spanish Renaissance. The bell tower dates from later and its chimes can be heard all over town.

Also on the Plaza Mayor is the **Museo Arqueológico** ⓘ *daily 1100-1400, 1600-1830 (1830-2000 summer), €3*, housed in a palace that also contains the tourist office (same opening hours). The museum has a replica of the colourful Dama de Baza as well as a comprehensive prehistoric section, some Roman architectural and ceramic remains and artefacts from the Moorish period.

Above the Colegiata, the **Moorish Alcazaba** is now a concrete compound that offers nothing more than views and a heavily restored section of Renaissance colonnade.

Where to stay

€€€ Cuevas Al Jatib
Arroyo Cúrcal s/n, T958-342248,
www.aljatib.com.

The Rolls Royce of troglodyte accommodation in Granada province, this sumptuous complex takes the humble cave into luxury class – has humanity gone full circle? The self-catering caves are appealing – although no more so than others in the area – but it's the classy restaurant, and, most of all, the cave-built hammam that sets this apart. Caves come in various sizes. Romantic, out-of-the-way and fun. Set a little way east of Baza, along the Camino de Oría; take the 'Baza este' exit from the motorway.

€ Hotel Anabel
C María de Luna s/n, a short walk to west of the centre, T958-860998, www. hotelanabelbaza.com.

Central Baza's best option, this hotel is situated above a vast restaurant (*menú del día* very reasonable). The rooms are well decorated with pale wooden floorboards, gratifyingly large beds and well-equipped bathrooms. There's also a lift and easy parking outside.

Restaurants

€€ Los Cántaros
C Arcipreste Juan Hernández s/n, T958-700375, www.restaurantelos cantaros.com.

Baza's best eating option, in the centre of town behind the cinema, combines a long bar stocked with happy tapas-eaters and an elegant dining area with round tables. There's good seafood on offer here – *quisquillas* (miniature shrimp) are worth trying, but it's hard to resist the allure of the wood-fired grill smoking away up the back. The steaks are excellent, but vegetarians are also well catered for with the house salad plump with avocado and artichokes.

€ La Solana
C Serrano 4, T958-861523, up a narrow lane off the Plaza Mayor.

The town's most characterful tapas bar. Packed floor to ceiling with curios, it's a warm and welcoming place. There's a wide choice of *raciones*; recommended are the brochettes, or the grilled cuttlefish.

Festivals

6-15 Sep Baza's **fiesta** is a lively event drawing villagers of the northeast of the province, as well as from Granada and Guadix.

Transport

Bus
Baza's bus station is on C Reyes Católicos, a short way east of the centre. There are hourly buses to **Granada** (1 hr 30 mins) via **Guadix** (30 mins), and there are 3 daily buses to **Huéscar** (1 hr), which continue to **Puebla de Don Fadrique**. There are 2-3 connections to **Almería** and **Jaén** daily: these require a change at Guadix, but the ongoing bus waits for you. There are also daily buses to **Madrid**, **Sevilla** and **Murcia**.

La Costa Tropical

★The short coastline of Granada province is a breath of fresh air between the Costa del Sol and the relentless plasticulture of western Almería province. Known as the Costa Tropical, it indeed has a fabulous climate, which is being increasingly sought by northern Europeans. The beach towns of La Herradura, Almuñécar and Salobreña are attractive places to stay.

Almuñécar and La Herradura

laid-back neighbouring beach towns

Almuñécar is a peaceful resort except in high summer, when its population multiplies by about eight times and it becomes a party capital for *granadinos* and *madrileños*. While the town still has plenty of Spanish character, it's increasingly being taken over by the expat invasion.

Almuñécar was founded as a trading outpost in the eighth century BC by the Phoenicians, who named it Sexi, inadvertently giving today's tourist board a mountain of marketing opportunities. Later a Roman town, it was renamed *Al-Munakkah* by the Moors. In AD 755, the Ummayad prince Abd al-Rahman arrived here after fleeing the massacre of his family in Damascus. He established himself in Córdoba, which under him began its pre-eminence in the western world. The town achieved more recent fame as the town where Laurie Lee fetched up after walking across Spain. His time here is described in *As I Walked Out One Midsummer Morning*; until Franco's death editions disguised the town as Castillo because it had been a hotbed of anarchist and republican sympathizers. When the Civil War started, Lee was picked up by a British destroyer and taken home. *A Rose for Winter* describes his return here after the war.

The **tourist office** ⓘ *Av de Europa s/n, T958-631125, www.turismoalmunecar.es, daily 0930-1330, 1630-1900 (1700-2000 in summer)*, stands in a striking neo-Moorish *palacio* just back from the Playa de San Cristóbal. There's also a tourist kiosk on the Paseo del Altillo between the old town and the beach.

Down the road from the tourist office is the **botanic gardens**, in the centre of which are the ruins of a Carthaginian and Roman factory for the making of the prized fish sauce called *garum*. The ruins are a little difficult to understand, but you can see the tanks where the fish was fermented. Around the gardens are small art workshops, one named for each province of Andalucía. Some of them run short courses in traditional handicrafts of the region.

Above here is the **castle** ① *Tue-Sat 1030-1330, 1600-1830 (1700-1930 summer), Sun 1000-1400, €2.35 joint entry with Museo Arqueológico.* It was originally fortified by the Phoenicians and then used by the Carthaginians and Romans. The Moorish rulers of Granada, the Nasrids, used it as a summer palace and a dungeon for political opponents. Heavily modified by Charles V in the 16th century, the castle was virtually destroyed during the Peninsular War. Until recently it was used as the town's cemetery. There's not a huge amount remaining inside, but some Moorish wall is preserved, as well as a scary dungeon. A small display of artefacts is housed in the central building, including an excellent bronze lion's head with the horns of a goat from the Roman period. There's also a scale model of the area, showing the locations of various ancient sites. Beyond here are some simple Roman tombs. The castle offers spectacular views both ways along the coast.

The **Museo Arqueológico** ① *C Málaga s/n, hours and admission as castle, above,* is housed in reconstructed Roman cisterns dating from the first century AD. Various finds are displayed, but the highlight is a fine Egyptian vase from around 1700 BC, with hieroglyphic inscriptions referring to the pharaoh Apophis/Apepi I, of whom almost nothing is known as he is associated with the mysterious Hyksos period. Its presence here is a mystery; best guess is that the Phoenicians brought it here a millennium after its manufacture. The staff here can tell you about more sites in the area, including various sections of Roman aqueducts and a Phoenician and Roman necropolis a 20-minute walk west of town.

Acuario de Almuñécar ① *Pl Kuwait s/n, T902-109835, www.acuarioalmunecar. es, 1000-1400, 1600-2000, hours change significantly through year, €12, children €9,* is the town's aquarium, a good two-level display of all that swims, sprouts and scuttles under the surface of the Mediterranean. There's information on underwater evolution and adaptation to the marine environment, as well as the obligatory tunnel where you can watch sharks, rays, and sunfish cruising about.

Loro Sexi (Sexy Parrot) ① *C Bikini s/n, open 1030-1400, 1600-1800 (1700-2000 summer), €4,* is a bird park in the middle of town, near the Playa San Cristóbal. There's a very good collection of parrots and their like, but many appear depressed and spend their time pulling their own feathers out. The macaws are particularly fine though, and other attractions include prim mandarin ducks, and striking silver and gold pheasants. The park is shady and makes an enjoyable stroll up and down the hillside.

The central town beach is **Playa Puerta del Mar**, where on the promenade is an imaginative monument to the Phoenicians and, nearby, a homage to Laurie Lee. A rocky outcrop, with a mirador and numerous seabirds, divides this from the better **Playa de San Cristóbal** to the west, which is backed by hotels and restaurants.

West of Almuñécar is the resort village of La Herradura. Between the two, there's some pleasant strolling to be done around the cliffs of the **Punta de la Mona**. The area's very popular for paragliding, and there are several good beaches around here, including **Playa El Muerto**, a relaxed and secluded nudist beach (nudism is mainstream in Spain).

La Herradura is a friendly, low-key place set around a large, sheltered bay with an attractive (if pebbly) beach. In the summer, it's busy with foreign and Spanish beachgoers, but its seafront *chiringuito* bars are still a perfect spot for a cold beer and plate of *boquerones fritos* on a hot day. Just out of La Herradura on the way to Nerja is a protected area, the Acantilados de Maro–Cerro Gordo, with spectacular cliffs, stunning views along the coast and secluded rocky coves with sandy beaches.

Listings Almuñécar and La Herradura

Where to stay

Almuñécar

There are numerous resort hotels along the Playa de San Cristóbal beach. Book ahead in summer. There are good off-season rates.

€€ Hostal Altamar
C Alta del Mar s/n, T958-630346, www.hostalaltamar.com.
Central spot with clean and well-kept rooms in the heart of the old town. It's not bad value in summer, but in winter it's an absolute bargain.

€€ Hotel Casablanca
Plaza San Cristóbal 4, T958-635575, www.hotelcasablanca almunecar.com.
In extravagant neo-Moorish style, this hotel is great value, especially off season and is a pebble's throw from the beach. Rooms are elegant, spacious, a/c, and many have balconies overlooking the sea. The bathrooms are decked out in black marble, and there's also a good restaurant.

€ Hostal Rocamar
C Córdoba 3, T958-630023.
Great value for money, this *hostal* is in the heart of things just off Av Andalucía and run by a friendly young family. Its rooms are decent for the price, and include a small bathroom. Very cheap off season.

Restaurants

Almuñécar

Just off Plaza Madrid, C Buenos Aires leads into a small square, Plaza Kelibia, surrounded by bars. They're all based half-outdoors and serve generous free snacks with each drink.

€€ Los Geraneos
Pl de la Rosa 4, T958-634020.
In a little square just off the waterfront promenade, this is a sweet place offering tasty meals, including a good Caesar salad and delicious fried brie with strawberry sauce.

€€ Mesón Gala
Pl Antonio Gala 5, T958-881455.
Deservedly popular indoor-outdoor venue with a boss who looks after his customers. Generous, interesting plates of free tapas accompany your drink, and tasty full meals never disappoint.

€ Bodega Francisco I
C Real 7.
Stocked with old photos and venerable barrels from which they draw excellent local wines, this bar could appear to be living in the past. But an upbeat attitude, tasty *raciones* and daily *menú*, as well as optimistic Southeast Asian art on the walls mean it's unique and usually packed at mealtimes. They also run a worthwhile meat restaurant further down the street.

€ La Trastienda
Plaza Kelibia s/n.
One of a clutch of appealing tapas bars on this square, this has a large terrace, an attractive indoor-outdoor bar area, and sound staff. There's a fine choice of *raciones*, including *roscas* (ring-shaped loaves of bread filled with *jamón serrano* and cheese), for sharing.

Bars and clubs

Almuñécar
There are 4 or 5 bars on the beach itself, below the Paseo; these get busy in summer with pumping music until late. The *discoteca* action mainly heats up during summer.

Festivals

Almuñécar
Jul Almuñécar hosts a significant **jazz festival** that attracts performers from around the world. Information on programming and ticketing can be found on the town's website, www.almunecar.info.

What to do

Almuñécar
Almuñécar Dive Center, *Paseo de Cotobro s/n, T958-634512, www.scubasur. com.* Run diving courses.
Centro Hípico Taramay, *behind the Hotel Taramay, T609-568966.* Can arrange horse-riding excursions in the area.

Transport

Almuñécar
Almuñécar has good bus connections. They stop at the bus station, a short walk northeast of the centre. Departures are nearly hourly to **Salobreña** and **Motril** (15 mins/30 mins). **Granada** is served by 8 to 9 daily buses (1 hr 15 mins) and other regular destinations include **Málaga** (1 hr 45 mins), some via **Nerja**; and **Almería** (3 hrs 10 mins).

Salobreña

picturesque white village cascading down a hill to the beach

Dominated by a Moorish castle and once an important Phoenician settlement, inviting Salobreña comprises a hilltop village which extends down past sugarcane plantations to its modern beachside extension. The planting of sugar ensures Salobreña's continued prosperity; indeed it's the only town in Europe with a sugar cane factory, the chimney of which you can see on the west side of town. With the old town preserving its Moorish street plan, and the beachside development fairly restrained, Salobreña is as quiet and pleasant a location as you could wish for.

The town's **tourist office** ① *Plaza de Goya, T958-610314, turismo@ayto-salobrena. org, Mon-Fri 0900-1500, 1630-2000, Sat-Sun 1000-1330,* is below the old town, on the roundabout just as you enter Salobreña if coming off the highway. You can download a guide to the town to your mobile phone.

The major sight is the **Castillo** ① *winter Tue-Sun 1000-1300, 1600-1900; summer daily 1000-1400, 1730-2115, €2.75, or €3.45 including the archaeological museum Museo Villa de Salobreña (same opening hours) on Plaza del Ayuntamiento.* Although fortified by successive occupying civilizations, the castle now dates mainly from the 12th century. It was used by Granada's Nasrid rulers as a palace and a prison, and still preserves much of its structure from this period. With steep cliffs on three sides, the only approach was through the houses, making it very siege resistant, especially as a fountain within the castle gave a reliable water supply. It is kidney shaped and consists of two enclosures, one of which contained the prison, which at one time or another held a number of disgraced Moorish kings such as Muley Hacen and Yusef III. A large flattened tower contained the armoury, while another tower protected the entrance. The Tower of Homage is of square construction and contains two large rooms on two storeys. The windows have decorated arches, and Moorish ceramics and glass have been found on the site. The views are exceptional from the walls.

The town's real pleasure is walking its steep narrow streets, which in parts suddenly give way to spectacular views from sheer drops. The beach is pretty good, and the development around it hasn't spoiled it. A string of bars and eateries along it make fine places for lunch on a hot day or for an evening drink while watching the spectacular sunsets.

Listings Salobreña

Where to stay

There are also various unexceptional mid-range hotels.

€€ Hostal Jayma
C Cristo 24, T958-610231, www. hostaljayma.com.
This *hostal* offers a big welcome and great modern rooms, all with terrace or balcony. The place is spotless, with excellent bathrooms and thoughtful extras like free bottled water. There's also a roof terrace with castle views. It's a great base in the old town, and well signposted. Recommended.

€ Pensión Mari Carmen
C Nueva 30, T958-610906, www. pensionmaricarmen.com.
A simple place with a friendly owner and a terrace with views over the sea. The decor is charming and the rooms, although without frills, are

very likeable. Rooms without bathroom are much cheaper.

Restaurants

The best places to eat are on the beachfront, with its terraced cafés, restaurants and bars.

€€ Casa Emilio
Paseo Marítimo 5, T958-349432, www. chiringuitocasaemilio.es.
One of the best of the seaside options, this is right on the beach with a great selection of grilled fish as well as rice dishes and their famous sardine skewers.

Transport

Bus
Buses run regularly from opposite the tourist office. See Almuñécar for routes and distances, which are practically the same.

West from Granada

West of Granada, the motorway speeds into the distance. It's worth taking a bit of time, however, to appreciate two excellent Spanish villages, Alhama de Granada and Montefrío.

Montefrío

dramatic setting in a craggy valley

This village 30 km north of the main road has a far-flung allure. A high limestone outcrop dominates the town, topped by a church. It's particularly striking at night, when the building is floodlit and seems to float in the air above the town.

The building is called the **Iglesia de la Villa**, and is built inside the old Moorish castle. Attractively early Renaissance in style; it has a **display** ⓘ *Mon-Fri 1200-1400*, on the Moorish culture of the region inside. The town itself is centred around the vast round neoclassical **Iglesia de la Encarnación**, which looks distinctly mosque-like from above. Its interior is a stunning space under the vast bare dome. Nearby is the helpful **tourist office** ⓘ *T958-336004*, in the Casa de Oficios.

Accessed from the road to Illora, **Las Peñas de los Gitanos** (Hills of the Gypsies) is an area of striking natural beauty, with grassy meadows dividing zones of olive trees and low Mediterranean forest. The *peñas* themselves are craggy limestone outcrops. The area harbours archaeological sites; caves occupied in the Neolithic era, several Chalcolithic necropolises with dolmens and the remains of Iberian and Visigothic see below. It's a wonderful area to lose yourself strolling around for a day.

From Montefrío, you have the options of heading east to Alcalá and Jaén province, or north into the Sistema Subbética of southern Córdoba.

Listings Montefrío

Where to stay

Ask at the tourist office for locals who sometimes have rooms available. There are several *casas rurales*; contact the tourist office or search online for information.

€€ Hotel La Enrea
Paraje de Enrea s/n, T958-336662,
www.laenreahotel.com.

At the entrance to the village, by a stream, this good-value hotel is in a former olive mill. There's a patio, a good restaurant and a lounge with a cosy fire.

Transport

Bus
3 buses run Mon-Sat between **Granada** and Montefrío (1 hr) ; there's also a daily bus to **Alcalá la Real** in Jaén province.

Alhama de Granada is perched on the edge of low cliffs dropping to a grassy ravine. The Moors named it for its natural hot springs. When the governor of the town was away in 1482, Christian forces took Alhama in a bloody battle; his lamenting cry "Ay! De mi Alhama!" is still used as an expression of regret.

The small 19th-century castle incorporates part of the original Moorish fortress but is a private residence. The **tourist office** ① *Carrera de Francisco de Toledo 10, T958-360686, www.turismodealhama.com, Mon 0930-1500, Tue-Fri 0930-1500, 1630-1830, Sat and Sun 1000-1430, 1630-1830*, is on the Paseo near it. Beyond here is the Iglesia del Carmen, from behind which you get excellent views of the *tajo* (ravine).

The church, **Santa María de la Encarnación**, is a chunky Gothic structure erected shortly after the reconquest of the town. Legend has it that the ornate vestments in the interior were embroidered by Isabel herself. The church was designed by Diego de Siloé among others. An inscription by one door commemorates King Alfonso XII helping victims of the 1884 earthquake, which killed 745 people in this region.

The **Moorish baths** ① *daily 1400-1600, €1, free Mon, closed mid-Dec to March*, are well preserved inside the Hotel Balneario, see below. A popular spot for a free hot bath is outside the entrance, where hot waters meet the river.

Listings Alhama de Granada

Where to stay

€€ Hotel Balneario
Ctra del Balneario s/n, 1 km from the centre, T958-350011, www.balnearioalhamade granada.com. Closed mid-Dec to Mar.
This spa hotel sits atop the natural hot springs. Rooms are large and comfy, and there are treatments. Could do with a spruce-up.

€€ La Seguiriya
C Las Peñas 12, T958-360636, www.laseguiriya.com.
Charmingly restored 18th-century house. Comfy rooms are named after flamenco singers. There's a terrace with views; includes breakfast. Recommended.

€ Pensión San José
Plaza de la Constitución 27, T958-350156, www.sanjosealhama.com.
An excellent budget option in the town centre, with a restaurant.

Restaurants

€ Bar Ochoa
Plaza San Sebastián s/n. Closed Tue.
Bursting with character: people always seem to be having a good time. That's largely down to the energetic owner and his *raciones* of local produce. Recommended.

Transport

Bus
There are 3 daily buses to **Granada**.

Background
Andalucía

History

Spain's proximity to Africa meant that Andalucía was one of Europe's frontlines for migrating hominids from the south. Discoveries near Burgos, in Spain's north attest that prehistoric humans inhabited the peninsula 1.3 million years ago; these are the oldest known hominid remains in Western Europe. Andalucía was a likely entry point.

One of the most important prehistoric European finds was discovered in **Gibraltar**; the finding of a woman's skull in one of the enclave's numerous caves was the first evidence of Neanderthals. The fossilized cranium has been dated to some 60,000 years.

While these fragments from an inconceivably distant past do little more than tantalize, there is substantial archaeological evidence of extensive occupation of Andalucía in the Upper Palaeolithic period. Several caves across the region have painting dating from this period, such as **La Pileta** near Ronda, and **Nerja** on the Málaga coast. Although not as sophisticated as the roughly contemporary works at Altamira in northern Spain, the depictions of horses, deer, fish and other animals are almost 20,000 years old and give a valuable insight into the lives of these early groups.

In 6000 BC, waves of immigration in the Almería area seem to have to ushered southern Spain rapidly into the Neolithic era. The Granada archaeological museum (see page 23), has some stunning finds from the **Cueva de los Murciélagos** in the south of the province, where burial goods include finely worked gold jewellery and some happily preserved woven *esparto* objects. From the same period are a new series of cave paintings at sites such as the **Cueva de los Letreros** near Vélez Blanco; one of the motifs here is the *Indalo*, a stick figure that was still used in the region until relatively recently as protection against evil spirits.

Around the middle of the third millennium, megalithic architecture began to appear in the form of dolmens, stone burial chambers whose most impressive exemplars are the massive structures at **Antequera**. At around the same time, the site of **Los Millares** in Almería province reveals a thriving and expanding society with an economy based on animal husbandry and working of copper; there is clear evidence of some form of contact with other Mediterranean peoples.

The Almería area is in a favoured geographical position for this type of cultural interchange, and it is no coincidence that the peninsula's first Bronze Age culture, known as **Agaric**, emerged in this region. Although almost nothing remains of the hilltop settlements themselves, excavations have retrieved bronze artefacts of a high technical standard and material that suggests extensive sea trading networks around the beginning of 2000 BC.

Around the turn of the first millennium, the face of the region was changing significantly. The people named as **Iberians** in later texts, and probably of local origin, inhabited the area and were joined by some **Celts**, although these peoples predominantly settled in the north of the peninsula. The Iberians had two distinct languages, unrelated to the Indo-European family, and benefited significantly from the arrival of another group, the **Phoenicians**.

These master sailors and merchants from the Levant set up many trading stations on the Andalucían coast. These included modern Huelva, Málaga and Cádiz; the latter, which they named **Gadir**, was possibly founded around 1100 BC, which would make it Western Europe's most venerable city. The Phoenicians set about trading with the Iberians, and began extensive mining operations, extracting gold, silver and copper from Andalucía's richly endowed soils.

Profitable contact with this maritime superpower led to the emergence of the wealthy local **Tartessian** civilization. Famed in classical sources as a mystical region where demigods walked streets paved with gold, precious little is actually known about this culture. Although they developed writing, it is undeciphered. Although it seems that they had an efficiently controlled society, no site worthy of being identified as the capital, Tartessos, has been excavated. Seemingly based in the region around the Guadalquivir valley, including in such settlements as Carmona, Niebla and Huelva, the Tartessians were highly skilled craftsmen; the Carambolo hoard found in Sevilla province consists of astonishingly intricate and beautiful gold jewellery.

Towards the end of the sixth century BC, the Tartessian culture seems to disappear and Iberian settlements appear to have reverted to self-governing towns, usually fortified places on hilltops. Continued contact with the Mediterranean, including with the **Greeks**, who had a brief presence on Spanish shores in the middle of the millennium, meant that these towns produced coins, texts and, particularly, fine sculpture, including such examples as the Dama de Baza, a lifesize seated goddess found in Granada province, and the Porcuna sculptures displayed in the provincial museum in Jaén.

As Phoenician power waned, their heirs and descendants, the **Carthaginians**, increased their operations in the western Mediterranean and settled throughout Andalucía, particularly at Cádiz. While the Phoenicians had enjoyed a mostly prosperous and peaceful relationship with the local peoples, the Carthaginians were more concerned with conquest and, under **Hamilcar Barca** and his relatives **Hasdrubal** and **Hannibal**, they took control of much of southern Spain and increased mining operations. The Iberian tribes, who included the **Turdetanians**, the group that had inherited the Tartessian mantle in the Guadalquivir basin, seem to have had mixed relations with the Barcid rulers. Some towns accepted Carthaginian control, while others resisted it.

Hispania

The Romans were bent on ending Punic power in the Mediterranean and soon realized that the peninsula was rapidly becoming a second Carthage. Roman troops arrived in Spain in 218 BC and Andalucía became one of the major theatres of the Second Punic War. Some of the local tribes, such as the Turdetanians, sided with the Romans against the Carthaginians and the final Roman victory came in

206 BC, at the Battle of Ilipa near Sevilla. The Carthaginians were kicked out of the peninsula.

During the war, the Romans had established the city of Itálica near Sevilla as a rest camp for dissatisfied Italian troops but it was only some time after the end of hostilities that the Romans appear to have developed an interest in the peninsula itself. Realizing the vast resources of the region, they set about conquering the whole of Hispania, a feat that they did not accomplish until late in the first century BC. It was the Romans that first created the idea of Spain as a single geographical entity, a concept it has struggled with ever since.

Rome initially divided the peninsula into two provinces, **Hispania Citerior** in the north and **Hispania Ulterior** in the south. Here, the military faced immediate problems from their one-time allies, the Turdetanians, who were not happy that the invaders hadn't returned home after defeating the Carthaginians. This rebellion was quelled brutally by Cato the Elder around 195 BC and, although there were several uprisings over the succeeding centuries, the Romans had far fewer problems in Andalucía than in the rest of the peninsula.

Part of this was due to the region's wealth. The ever-increasing mining operations mostly used slave labour and gave little back to the locals, but exports of olive oil, wine and *garum* meant the local economy thrived, despite the heavy tributes exacted by the Republic. Roman customs rubbed off on the Iberians and the local languages gradually disappeared as Latin became predominant.

The wealth of Hispania meant that it became an important pawn in the power struggles of the Roman republic and it was in Andalucía, near modern Bailén, that **Julius Caesar** finally defeated Pompey's forces in 45 BC. With peace established, Caesar set about establishing colonies in earnest; many of Andalucía's towns and cities were built or rebuilt by the Romans in this period. Julius knew the region pretty well; he had campaigned here in 68 BC and later had been governor of Hispania Ulterior. The contacts he had made during this period served him well and Caesar rewarded the towns that had helped him against Pompey, such as Sevilla and Cádiz, by conferring full Roman citizenship on the inhabitants. Later, Vespasian granted these rights to the whole of the peninsula.

Augustus redivided Hispania into three provinces; the southernmost, **Baetica**, roughly corresponded to modern Andalucía. Initially administered from Córdoba, the capital was switched to Hispalis (Sevilla), which, along with neighbouring Itálica, prospered under the Imperial regime. The south of Spain became a real Roman heartland, the most Roman of the Roman colonies. Itálica was the birthplace of the Emperor Trajan and sometime home of his protegé Hadrian, while the Seneca family originated in Córdoba. The first century AD was a time of much peace and prosperity and Andalucía's grandest Roman remains date largely from this period.

It was probably during this century that the bustling Andalucían ports heard their first whisperings of Christianity, which arrived early in the peninsula. Around this time, too, a Jewish population began to build up; the beginnings of what was a crucial segment of Andalucían society for 1500 years.

A gradual decline began late in the second century AD, with raids from North Africa nibbling at the edges of a weakening empire. The Iberian provinces took the wrong side in struggles for the emperorship and suffered as a result; by the fourth century, Cádiz was virtually in ruins and the lack of control meant that an almost feudal system developed, with wealthy citizens controlling local production from fortified villas. Christianity had become a dominant force, but religious squabblings exacerbated rather than eased the tension.

In the fifth century, as the Roman order tottered, various barbarian groups streamed across the Pyrenees and created havoc. **Alans** and **Vandals** established themselves in the south of Spain; it has been (almost certainly erroneously) suggested that the latter group lent their name to Andalucía. The Romans enlisted the Visigoths to restore order on their behalf. This they succeeded in doing, but they liked the look of the land and returned for good after they lost control of their French territories. After a period of much destruction and chaos, a fairly tenuous Visigothic control ensued. They used Sevilla as an early capital, but later transferred their seat of power to Toledo.

The Visigoths

While there is little enough archaeological and historical evidence from this period, what has been found shows that the Visigoths had inherited Roman customs and architecture to a large degree, while many finds exhibit highly sophisticated carving and metalworking techniques. The bishop and writer San Isidoro produced some of Europe's most important post-Roman texts from his base in Sevilla. There were likely comparatively few Visigoths; a small warrior class ruling with military strength best fits the evidence, and they seem to have fairly rapidly become absorbed into the local culture.

The politics of the Visigothic period are characterized by kinstrife and wranglings over Christian doctrine. Some of the numerous dynastic struggles were fought across a religious divide: the Visigothic monarchs were initially adherents of Arianism, a branch of Christianity that denied the coëval status of the Son in the Trinity. While the general population was Catholic, this wasn't necessarily a major stumbling block, but various pretenders to the throne used the theological question as a means for gaining support for a usurpment. During these struggles in the mid-sixth century, various of the pretenders called upon Byzantine support and Emperor Justinian I took advantage of the situation to annex the entire Andalucían coastline as a province, which was held for some 70 years. Inland Andalucía had proved difficult to keep in line for the Visigothic monarchs: King Agila was defeated by a rising in Córdoba and the Sevilla-based businessman Athanagild managed to maneouvre his way on to the throne. He and his successor Leovigild finally pacified the unruly Córdobans, but Leovigild faced a revolt in Andalucía from his own son, Hermenegild, who had converted to Catholicism. Father defeated offspring and the kingdom passed to Leovigild's younger son Reccared (AD 586-601), who wisely converted to Catholicism and established a period of relative peace and prosperity for the people of the peninsula.

BACKGROUND

San Isidoro

"No one can gain a full understanding of Spain without a knowledge of Saint Isidore" - Richard Ford

Born in AD 560, Isidoro succeeded his brother Leandro as Bishop of Sevilla. One of the most important intellectual figures of the Middle Ages, his prolific writings cover all subjects and were still popular at the time of the Renaissance. His *Etymologiae* was one of the first secular books in print when it appeared in AD 1472. The first encyclopedia written in the Christian west, it became the primary source for the 154 classical authors that Isidoro quoted. He also wrote on music, law, history and jurisprudence as well as doctrinal matters.

Isidoro is also recognized as an important church reformer and was responsible for the production of the so-called Mozarabic rite which is still practised in Toledo Cathedral today. His writings were an attempt to restore vigour and direction to a church that was in decline following the Visigothic invasions.

Another important element to Isidoro's writings were his prophecies, based both on the Bible and classical references. This element of his writings appealed to later generations living in the shadow of the Muslim conquests and was to be the source of many stories and legends. Following the expulsion of the Moors it seemed to some that an ancient prophecy was about to be fulfilled.

Isidoro died in Sevilla in AD 636 and his writings continued to inspire Spain for the next nine centuries. His body is now in León, moved there by Fernando I of Castilla who repatriated it to the Christian north around AD 1060.

The seventh century saw numerous changes of rulers, many of whom imposed increasingly severe strictures on the substantial Jewish population of the peninsula. Restrictions on owning property, attempted forced conversions and other impositions foreshadowed much later events in Spain. The Visigoths possibly paid a heavy price for this persecution; several historians opine that the Moorish invasion was substantially aided by the support of Jewish communities that (rightly, as it turned out) viewed the conquerors as liberators.

Al-Andalus

In AD 711 an event occurred that was to define Spanish history for the next eight centuries. The teachings of Mohammed had swept across North Africa and the Moors were to take most of Spain before the prophet had been dead for even a century. After a number of exploratory raids, Tarik, governor of Tanger, crossed the straits with a small force of mostly Berber soldiers. It is said that he named the large rock he found after himself; Jebel Tarik (the mountain of Tarik), a name which over time evolved into Gibraltar. Joined by a larger force under the command of the governor of North Africa, Musa ibn-Nusair, the Moors then defeated and slew the Visigothic king Roderic somewhere near Tarifa. The conquests continued under Musa's son Abd al-Aziz until almost the whole peninsula was in Moorish hands: the conquest had taken less than three years, an extraordinary feat. Soon the Muslim armies were well advanced on the *autoroutes* of southern France.

The Moors named their Iberian dominions Al-Andalus and while these lands grew and shrunk over time, the heartland was always in the south. After the conquest, Al-Andalus was administered by governors based in Córdoba, who ultimately answered to the Ummayad caliph in distant Damascus. This shift of the effective capital south from Toledo to Córdoba meant that the peninsula's focus was much more in Andalucía and, consequently, the Mediterranean and North Africa.

In AD 750, an event occurred in distant Damascus that was to shape the destiny of Moorish Spain. The Abbasid dynasty ousted the ruling Umayyad family and proceeded to massacre them. One prince, Abd al-Rahman, managed to escape the carnage and made his way to Spain in AD 756. Arriving in Córdoba, he contrived to gain and hold power in the city. Gradually taking control over more and more of Al-Andalus, he established the emirate of Córdoba, which was to rule the Moorish dominions in Spain for nearly three centuries.

Romantic depictions of Al-Andalus as a multicultural paradise are way off the mark; the situation is best described by Richard Fletcher as one of "grudging toleration, but toleration nonetheless". Christians and Jews were allowed relative freedom of worship and examples of persecution are comparatively few. Moorish texts throughout the history of Al-Andalus reveal a condescending attitude towards non-Muslims (and vice-versa in Christian parts of Spain), but it is probable that in day-to-day life there was large-scale cultural contact, a process described by Spanish historians as *convivencia* (cohabitation). The conversion of Christians and Jews to Islam was a gradual but constant process; this was no doubt given additional impetus by the fact that Muslims didn't pay any tax beyond the alms required as part of their faith. Christian converts to Islam were known as *muwallads*, while those who remained Christian under the rule of the Moors are called *mozárabes* or Mozarabs.

Arabic rapidly became the major language of southern Spain, even among non-Muslims. The number of Arabic words in modern Spanish attests to this. Many of them refer to agriculture and crops; the Moors brought with them vastly improved farming and irrigation methods, as well as a host of fruits and vegetables not grown before on the peninsula's soil. This, combined with wide and profitable trading routes in the Mediterranean, meant that Al-Andalus began to thrive economically, which must have assisted in the pacification of the region. Córdoba's Mezquita, begun in the eighth century, was expanded and made richer in various phases through this period; this can be seen as reflecting both the growing wealth and the increasing number of worshippers.

Geography divides Spain into distinct regions, which have tended to persist through time, and it was one of these – Asturias – that the Moors had trouble with. They were defeated in what was presumably a minor skirmish in AD 717 at Covadonga, in the far northern mountains. While the Moors weren't too rattled by this at the time, Spain views it today as a happening of immense significance, a victory against all odds and even a sort of mystical watershed where God proved himself to be on the Christian side. It was hardly a crippling blow to the Moors, but it probably sowed the seeds of what became the **Asturian** and **Leonese** monarchy. A curious development in many ways, this royal line emerged unconquered from the shadowy northern hills and forests. Whether they were a last bastion of Visigothic resistance, or whether they were just local folk ready to defend their lands, they established an organized little kingdom of sorts with a capital that shifted about but settled on Oviedo in AD 808.

The Asturian kingdom began to grow in strength and the long process of the *Reconquista*, the Christian reconquest of the peninsula, began. The northerners took advantage of cultural interchange with the south, which remained significant during the period despite the militarized zone in between, and were soon strong enough to begin pushing back. The loose Moorish authority in these lands certainly helped; the northern zone was more or less administered by warlords who were only partially controlled by the emirs and caliphs in Córdoba. Galicia and much of the north coast was reclaimed and in AD 914 the Asturian king Ordoño II reconquered León; the capital shortly moved to here and the line of kings took on the name of that town. As the Christians moved south, they re-settled many towns and villages that had lain in ruins since Roman times.

By the 10th century, the economy was booming in Córdoba and its dominions. A growing sophistication in politics and the arts was partly driven by cultured expats from Damascus and Baghdad who brought learning and fashions from the great cities of the Arab world. It was a time of achievement in literature, the sciences and engineering, including the works of classical writers such as Aristotle and Arabic treatises on subjects such as astronomy and engineering. The whole of Europe felt the benefit as knowledge permeated to the Christian north.

Little wonder then, that the emir Abd al-Rahman III (AD 912-961) felt in bullish mood. In AD 929 he gave himself the title of *caliph*, signalling a definitive break with the east as there can only be one caliph (ordained successor to Mohammed) and he was in Baghdad. Although he had no basis to name himself caliph, the declaration served to establish Al-Andalus as a free-standing Islamic kingdom in the west. Córdoba at this time probably had over 100,000 inhabitants, which would have put it at the same level as Constantinople and far above any other European city. Abd al-Rahman celebrated the new status by building an incredibly lavish palace and administration complex, **Madinat al-Zahra (Medina Azahara)**, to the west of the city.

But Asturias/León wasn't the only Christian power to have developed. The Basques had been quietly pushing outwards too and their small mountain

BACKGROUND

The Conqueror

Mohammed ibn-Abi al Ma'afari was born to a poor family near Algeciras around AD 938. Known to latter generations as Al-Manzur or 'the conqueror', he is one of the most remarkable figures of the Middle Ages, representing both the strength of Muslim Spain and its ultimate failure. A lawyer, he succeeded in reforming the administration of the Caliphate and in modernizing its army before getting his chance at power as one of three co-regents named to govern while the child-caliph Hisham II grew to maturity. Al-Manzur managed to manoeuvre the other co-regents out of the way, having one imprisoned and murdered and engaging the forces of the other in battle. Meanwhile, he beguiled Hisham with wine, women, and song so successfully that once the caliph grew up he never made a political decision, letting Al-Manzur rule in his stead. The regent was so sure of his position that he even took the title of king in AD 996.

While regent, he launched a series of lightning raids across the Christian north. His army, made up of mercenary Slavs, Christian renegades and North African Berbers, sacked Zamora and Simancas in AD 981, Barcelona in AD 985 and León in AD 987. The Leonese king Bermudo had broken an agreement to pay tribute and was forced to flee to the Asturian mountains. In AD 997 he embarked on his final campaign to extinguish Christian opposition. He took A Coruña and the holy city of Santiago where he removed the bells of the cathedral to the mosque of Córdoba. On encountering a lone priest protecting the shrine of St James he is said to have ordered his men to leave the holy relics of the city untouched.

While his military exploits were undoubtedly one of the period's great feats of generalship, Al-Manzur was not really a bloodthirsty tyrant. Under his guidance a university was established in Córdoba and he was a great patron of the arts and science. On his many military campaigns both in Spain and North Africa he took a library of books. It was under Al-Manzur that the final expansion of the Mezquita took place.

After an inconclusive battle in 1002 at Calatañazor in Castilla, Al-Manzur died of natural causes. The relief of the Christians was immense, even more so when the caliphate, without the Conqueror at the helm, disintegrated six years later.

kingdom of Navarra grew rapidly. Aragón emerged and gained power and size via a dynastic union with Catalunya. The entity that came to dominate Spain, Castilla, was born at this time too. In the middle of the 10th century, a Burgos noble, Fernán González, declared independence from the kingdom of León and began to rally disparate Christian groups in the region. He was so successful in this endeavour that it wasn't long before his successors labelled themselves kings.

Both the Christian and Muslim powers were painfully aware of their vulnerability and constructed a series of massive fortresses that faced each other across the central plains. The Muslim fortresses were particularly formidable; high eyries with commanding positions, accurately named the 'front teeth' of Al-Andalus. Relations between Christian and Muslim Spain were curious. While there were frequent campaigns, raids and battles, there was also a high level of peaceful contact and diplomacy. Even the fighting was far from being a confrontation of implacably opposed rivals: Christian knights and Moorish mercenaries hired themselves out to either side, none more so than the famous El Cid.

The caliphate faced a very real threat from the Fatimid dynasty in North Africa and campaigning in the Christian north was one way to fund the fortification of the Mediterranean coast. No-one campaigned more successfully than the formidable Al-Manzur (see box, opposite), who, while regent for the child-caliph Hisham II, conducted no fewer than 57 victorious sallies into the peninsula, succeeding in sacking almost every city in Northern Spain in a 30-year campaign of terror. Al-Manzur was succeeded by his equally adept son Abd al-Malik, but when he died young in 1008, the caliphate disintegrated with two rival Ummayad claimants seeking to fill the power vacuum.

Twenty years of civil war followed and Córdoba was more or less destroyed. Both sides employed a variety of Christian and Muslim mercenaries to prosecute their claims to the caliphal throne; the situation was bloody and chaotic in the extreme. When the latest puppet caliph was deposed in 1031, any pretence of centralized government evaporated and Berber generals, regional administrators and local opportunists seized power in towns across Al-Andalus, forming the small city-states known as the *taifa* kingdoms; *taifa* means faction in Arabic.

This first *taifa* period lasted for most of the rest of the 11th century and in many ways sounded an early death-knell for Muslim Spain. Petty rivalries between the neighbouring *taifas* led to recruitment of Christian military aid in exchange for large sums of cash. This influx led in turn to the strengthening of the northern kingdoms and many *taifas* were then forced to pay tribute, or protection money, to Christian rulers or face obliteration.

The major *taifas* in Andalucía were Sevilla and Granada, which gradually swallowed up several of their smaller neighbours. The Abbadid rulers of Sevilla led a hedonistic life, the kings Al-Mu'tadid and his son Al-Mu'tamid penning poetry between revelries and romantic liaisons. A pogrom against the Jewish population in 1066 indicated that there was little urban contentment behind the luxuriant façade.

The Christian north lost little time in taking advantage of the weak *taifa* states. As well as exacting punitive tribute, the Castilian king Alfonso VI had his eye on conquests and crossed far beyond the former frontline of the Duero valley. His capture of highly symbolic Toledo, the old Visigothic capital and Christian centre, in 1085, finally set alarm bells ringing in the verse-addled brains of the *taifa* kings.

They realized they needed help, and they called for it across the Straits to Morocco. Since the middle of the 11th century, a group of tribesmen known as the **Almoravids** had been establishing control there and their leader, Yusuf, was invited across to Al-Andalus to help combat Alfonso VI. A more unlikely alliance is hard to imagine; the Almoravids were barely-literate desert warriors with a strong and fundamentalist Islamic faith, a complete contrast to the *taifa* rulers in their blossom-scented pleasure domes. The Almoravid armies defeated Alfonso near Badajoz in 1086 but were appalled at the state of Islam in Al-Andalus, so Yusuf decided to stay and establish a stricter observance. He rapidly destroyed the *taifa* system and established governors, answerable to Marrakech, in the major towns, including Sevilla, having whisked the poet-king off to wistful confinement in Fez.

Almoravid rule was marked by a more aggressive approach to the Christian north, which was matched by the other side. Any hope of retaking much territory soon subsided, as rebellions from the local Andalusi and pressure from another dynasty, the Almohads in Morocco, soon took their toll. This was compounded by another factor: tempted no doubt by big lunches, tapas, siestas and free-poured spirits, the hardline Almoravids were lapsing into softer ways. Control again dissolved into local *taifas*; Alfonso VII took advantage, seizing Córdoba in 1146 and Almería in 1147.

They weren't held for long, though. The Almohads, who by now controlled Morocco, began crossing the Straits to intervene in Andalusi military affairs. Although similarly named and equally hard line in their Islamism, the Almohads were significantly different to the Almoravids, with a canny grasp of politics and advanced military tactics. They founded the settlement of Gibraltar in 1159, took back Almería and Córdoba and gained control over the whole of what is now Andalucía by about 1172. Much surviving military architecture in Andalucía was built by the Almohads, including the great walls and towers of Sevilla. Yet they too lapsed into decadence, and bungled planning led to the very costly military defeat at Las Navas de Tolosa at the hands of Alfonso VIII in 1212. This was a major blow. Alfonso's son Fernando III (1217-1252) capitalized on his father's success, taking Córdoba in 1236, Jaén, the 'Iron Gate' of Andalucía, in 1246, and then Sevilla, the Almohad capital, in 1248, after a two-year siege. The loss of the most important city of Al-Andalus, mourned across the whole Muslim world, was effectively the end of Moorish power in Spain, although the emirate of Granada lingered on for another 250 years. Fernando, sainted for his efforts, kicked out all Sevilla's Moorish inhabitants, setting a pattern of intolerance towards the *mudéjares*, as those Muslims who lived under Christian rule came to be called.

What was left of Muslim Spain was the emirate of Granada. The nobleman Mohammed Ibn-Yusuf Ibn-Nasr set himself up here as ruler in 1237 and gave his name to the Nasrid dynasty. Although nominally independent, it was to a large extent merely a vassal of the Castilian kings. Mohammed surrendered Jaén and began paying tribute to Fernando III in exchange for not being attacked in Granada. He even sent a detachment of troops to help besiege Sevilla, a humiliation that eloquently shows how little real power he had. His territory included a long stretch of the Andalucían coastline from the Atlantic eastwards past Almería and a small inland area that included Granada itself, Antequera and Ronda.

Meanwhile, the Christians were consolidating their hold on most of Andalucía, building churches and cathedrals over the mosques they found and trying to find settlers to work the vast new lands at their disposal as many of the Moors had fled to the kingdom of Granada or across the sea to North Africa. Nobles involved in the *Reconquista* claimed vast tracts of territory; estates known as *latifundias* that still exist today and that have been the cause of numerous social problems in Andalucía over the centuries.

The Christians still had some fighting to do. The Marinid rulers of Morocco were a constant menace and managed to take Algeciras in the late 13th century. Tarifa was recaptured in 1292 and became the scene of the famous heroic actions of Guzmán 'El Bueno' who defended it against another siege two years later. There were also regular, if half-hearted, Christian campaigns agaist Nasrid Granada, one of which involved Sir James 'the Black' Douglas, who met his death carrying the embalmed heart of Robert the Bruce into combat at Teba in 1329.

The Nasrid kingdom continued to survive, partly because its boundaries were extremely well fortified with a series of thousands of defensive towers. The Alhambra as we know it was mostly built under Mohammad V in the second half of the 14th century; at the same time, the enlightened Castilian king Pedro I was employing Moorish craftsmen to recreate Sevilla's Alcázar in sumptuous style.

The Golden Age

In the 15th century, there were regular rebellions and much kinstrife over succession in the Nasrid kingdom, which was beginning to seem ripe for the plucking. One of the reasons this hadn't yet happened was that the Christian kingdoms were involved in similar succession disputes. Then, in 1469, an event occurred that was to spell the end for the Moorish kingdom and have a massive impact on the history of the world. The heir to the Aragonese throne, Fernando, married Isabel, heiress of Castilla, in a secret ceremony in Valladolid. The implications were enormous. Aragón was still a power in the Mediterranean (Fernando was also king of Sicily) and Castilla's domain covered much of the peninsula. The unification under the *Reyes Católicos*, as the monarchs became known, marked the beginnings of Spain as we know it today. Things didn't go smoothly at first, however. There were plenty of opponents to the union and forces in support of Juana, Isabel's elder (but claimed by her to be illegitimate) sister waged wars across Castilla.

When the north was once more at peace, the monarchs found that they ruled the entire peninsula except for Portugal, with which a peace had just been negotiated, the small mountain kingdom of Navarra, which Fernando stood a decent chance of inheriting at some stage anyway, and the decidedly un-Catholic Nasrids in their sumptuous southern palaces. The writing was on the wall and Fernando and Isabel began their campaign. Taking Málaga in 1487 and Almería in 1490, they were soon at Granada's gates. The end came with a whimper, as the vacillating King Boabdil, who had briefly allied himself with the monarchs in a struggle against his father, elected not to go down fighting and surrendered the keys of the great city on New Year's Day in 1492 in exchange for a small principality in the Alpujarra region (which in the end he decided not to take and left for Morocco). His mother had little sympathy as he looked back longingly at the city he had left. "You weep like a woman," she allegedly scolded, "for what you could not defend like a man".

The Catholic Monarchs had put an end to Al-Andalus, which had endured in various forms for the best part of 800 years. They celebrated in true Christian style by kicking the Jews out of Spain. Andalucía's Jewish population had been hugely significant for a millennium and a half, heavily involved in commerce, shipping and literature throughout the peninsula. But hatred of them had begun to grow in the 14th century and there had been many pogroms, including an especially vicious one in 1391, which began in Sevilla and spread to most other cities in Christian Spain. Many converted during these years to escape the murderous atmosphere; they became known as *conversos*. The decision to expel those who hadn't converted was far more that of the pious Isabel than the pragmatic Fernando and has to be seen in the light of the paranoid Christianizing climate. The Jews were given four months to leave the kingdom and even the *conversos* soon found themselves under the iron hammer of the Inquisition.

The valleys of the Alpujarra region south of Granada were where many refugees from previously conquered Moorish areas had fled to from the Christians. When Granada itself fell, many Muslims came here to settle on the rich agricultural land. Although under the dominion of the Catholic Monarchs, it was still largely Muslim in character and it is no surprise that, as new anti-Islamic legislation began to bite, it was here that rebellion broke out. From 1499, the inhabitants fought the superior Christian armies for over two years until the revolt was bloodily put down. In no mood for conciliation, Fernando and Isabel gave the Moors the choice of baptism (converts became known as *moriscos*) or expulsion. Emigration wasn't feasible for most; a vast sum of money had to be handed over for the 'privilege' and in most cases parents weren't allowed to take their children with them.

There was another *morisco* revolt in 1568, again centred on the Alpujarra region. After this, there was forcible dispersal and resettlement of their population throughout Spain. Finally, the *moriscos* too were expelled (in 1609) by Felipe III. It is thought that the country lost some 300,000 of its population and parts of Spain have perhaps still not wholly recovered from this self-inflicted purge of the majority of its intellectual, commercial and professional talent. The lack of cultural diversity led to long-term stagnation. The ridiculous doctrine of *limpieza de sangre* (purity of blood) became all-important; the enduring popularity of pig meat surely owes something to these days, when openly eating these foods proved that one wasn't Muslim or Jewish.

But we move back for a moment to 1492. One of the crowd watching Boabdil hand the keys to Granada over to Fernando and Isabel was Cristóbal Colón (Christopher Columbus), who had been petitioning the royal couple for ships and funds to mount an expedition to sail westwards to the Indies. Finally granted his request, he set off from Palos de la Frontera near Huelva and, after a deal of hardship, reached what he thought was his goal. In the wake of Columbus's discovery, the treaty of Tordesillas in 1494 partitioned the Atlantic between Spain and Portugal and led to the era of Spanish colonization of the Americas. In many ways, this was an extension of the *Reconquista* as young men hardened on the Castilian and Extremaduran *meseta* crossed the seas with zeal for conquest, riches and land. Andalucía was both enriched and crippled by this exodus: while the cities flourished on the New World booty and trade, the countryside was denuded of people to work the land. The biggest winner proved to be Sevilla, which was granted a monopoly over New World trade by the Catholic Monarchs in 1503. It grew rapidly and became one of Western Europe's foremost cities. In 1519 another notable endeavour began here. Ferdinand Magellan set sail from Triana, via Sanlúcar de Barrameda, in an attempt to circumnavigate the world. He didn't make it, dying halfway, but one of the expedition's ships did. Skippered by a Basque, Juan Sebastián Elkano, it arrived some three years later.

Isabel died in 1504, but refused to settle her Castilian throne on her husband, Fernando, to his understandable annoyance, as the two had succeeded in uniting virtually the whole of modern Spain under their joint rule. The inheritance passed to their mad daughter, Juana la Loca, and her husband, Felipe of Burgundy (el Hermoso or the Fair), who came to Spain in 1506 to claim their inheritance. Felipe soon died, however, and his wife's obvious inability to govern led to Fernando being recalled as regent of the united Spain until the couple's son, Carlos, came of age. During this period Fernando completed the boundaries of modern Spain by annexing Navarra. On his deathbed he reluctantly agreed to name Carlos heir to Aragón and its territories, thus preserving the unity he and Isabel had forged. Carlos I of Spain (Carlos V) inherited vast tracts of European land; Spain and southern Italy from his maternal grandparents, and Austria, Burgundy and the Low Countries from his paternal ones. He was shortly named Holy Roman Emperor and if all that worldly power weren't enough, his friend, aide and tutor, Adrian of Utrecht, was soon elected Pope.

The first two Habsburg monarchs, Carlos V and then his son Felipe II relied on the income from the colonies to pursue wars (often unwillingly) on several European fronts. It couldn't last; Spain's Golden Age has been likened by historian Felipe Fernández-Armesto to a dog walking on its hind legs. While Sevilla prospered from the American expansion, the provinces declined, hastened by a drain of citizens to the New World. The *comunero* revolt expressed the frustrations of a region that was once the focus of optimistic Christian conquest and agricultural wealth, but had now become peripheral to the designs of a 'foreign' monarchy. Resentment was exacerbated by the fact that the king still found it difficult to extract taxes from the *cortes* of Aragón or Catalunya, so Castilla (of which Andalucía was a part) bankrolled a disproportionate amount of the crippling costs of the running of a worldwide empire. The growing administrative requirements of managing an empire had forced the previously itinerant Castilian monarchs to choose a capital and Felipe II picked the small town of Madrid in 1561, something of a surprise, as Sevilla or Valladolid were more obvious choices. Although central, Madrid was remote, tucked away behind a shield of hills in the interior. This seemed in keeping with the somewhat paranoid nature of Habsburg rule. And beyond all other things, they were paranoid about threats to the Catholic religion; the biggest of which, of course, they perceived to be Protestantism. This paranoia was costly in the extreme.

The struggle of the Spanish monarchy to control the spread of Protestantism was a major factor in the decline of the empire. Felipe II fought expensive and ultimately unwinnable wars in Flanders that bankrupted the state; while within the country the absolute ban on the works of heretical philosophers, scientists and theologists left Spain behind in Renaissance Europe. In the 18th century, for example, the so-called Age of Enlightenment in Western Europe, theologists at the noble old university of Salamanca debated what language the angels spoke; that Castilian was proposed as a likely answer is certain. Felipe II's successors didn't have his strength of character; Felipe III was ineffectual and dominated by his advisors, while Felipe IV, so sensitively portrayed by Velázquez, tried hard but was indecisive and unfortunate, despite the best efforts of his favourite, the remarkable Conde-Duque de Olivares. As well as being unwillingly involved in several costly wars overseas, there was also a major rebellion in Catalunya in the mid-17th century. The decline of the monarchy parallelled a physical decline in the monarchs, as the inbred Habsburgs became more and more deformed and weak; the last of them, Carlos II, was a tragic victim of contorted genetics who died childless and plunged the nation into a war of succession. "Castilla has made Spain and Castilla has destroyed it," commented early 20th century essayist José Ortega y Gasset. While the early 17th century saw the zenith of the Seville school of painting, the city was in decline; the expulsion of the *moriscos* had removed a vital labour force and merchants and bankers were packing up and going elsewhere as the crown's economic problems led to increasingly punitive taxation. The century saw several plagues in Andalucían cities and Sevilla lost an incredible half of its inhabitants in 1649.

The death of poor heirless Carlos II was a long time coming and foreign powers were circling to try and secure a favourable succession to the throne of Spain. Carlos eventually named the French duke Felipe de Bourbon as his successor, much to the concern of England and Holland, who declared war on France. War broke out throughout Spain until the conflict's eventual resolution at the Treaty of Utrecht; at which Britain received Gibraltar, and Spain also lost its Italian and Low Country possessions.

The Bourbon dynasty succeeded in bringing back a measure of stability and wealth to Spain in the 18th century. Sevilla's decline and the silting up of the Guadalquivir led to the monarchs establishing Cádiz as the centre for New World trade in its place and Spain's oldest city prospered again. The Catholic church, however, was in a poor state intellectually and came to rely more and more on cults and fiestas to keep up the interest of the populace: many of Andalucía's colourful religious celebrations were formed during this period. The 18th century also saw the energetic reformer Pedro de Olavide, chief adviser to King Carlos III, try to repopulate rural Andalucía by creating planned towns and encouraging foreign settlers to live in them.

The 19th century in Andalucía and Spain was turbulent to say the least. The 18th century had ended with a Spanish-French conflict in the wake of the French revolution. Peace was made after two years, but worse was to follow. First was a heavy defeat for a joint Spanish-French navy by Nelson off Cabo Trafalgar near Cádiz. Next Napoleon tricked Carlos IV. Partitioning Portugal between France and Spain seemed like a good idea to Spain, which had always coveted its western neighbour. It wasn't until the French armies seemed more interested in Madrid than Lisbon that Carlos IV got the message. Forced to abdicate in favour of his rebellious son Fernando, he was then summoned to a conference with Bonaparte at Bayonne, with his son, wife and Manuel Godoy, his able and trusted adviser (who is often said to have been loved even more by the queen than the king). Napoleon had his own brother Joseph (known among Spaniards as *Pepe Botellas* for his heavy drinking) installed on the throne.

On 2 May 1808 (still a red-letter day in Spain), the people revolted against this arrogant gesture and Napoleon sent in the troops later that year. Soon after, a hastily assembled Spanish army inflicted a stunning defeat on the French at Bailén, near Jaén; the Spaniards were then joined by British and Portuguese forces and the ensuing few years are known in Spain as the Guerra de Independencia (War of Independence). The allied forces under Wellington won important battles after the initiative had been taken by the French. The behaviour of both sides was brutal both on and off the battlefield. Marshal Soult's long retreat across the region saw him loot town after town; his men robbed tombs and burned priceless archives. The allied forces were little better; the men Wellington had referred to as the 'scum of the earth' sacked the towns they conquered with similar destructiveness.

Significant numbers of Spaniards had been in favour of the French invasion and were opposed to the liberal republican movements that sprang up in its wake. In 1812, a revolutionary council in Cádiz, on the point of falling to the French, drafted a constitution proclaiming a democratic parliamentary monarchy of sorts. Liberals had high hopes that this would be brought into effect at the end of the war, but the returning king, Fernando, revoked it. Meanwhile, Spain was on the point of losing its South American colonies, which were being mobilized under *libertadores* such as Simón Bolívar. Spain sent troops to restore control; a thankless assignment for the soldiers involved. One of the armies was preparing to leave Cádiz in 1820 when the commander, Rafael de Riego, invoked the 1812 constitution and refused to fight under the 'unconstitutional' monarchy. Much of the army joined him and the king was forced to recognize the legality of the constitution. Things soon dissolved though, with the 'liberals' (the first use of the word) being split into factions and opposed by the church and aristocracy. Eventually, king Fernando called on the king of France to send an invading army; the liberals were driven backwards to Sevilla, then to Cádiz, where they were defeated and Riego taken to his execution in Madrid. In many ways this conflict mirrored the later Spanish Civil War. Riego, who remained (and remains) a hero of the democratically minded, did not die in vain; his stand impelled much of Europe on the road to constitutional democracy, although it took Spain itself over a century and a half to find democratic stability.

The remainder of the century was to see clash after clash of liberals against conservatives, progressive cities against reactionary countryside, restrictive centre against outward-looking periphery. Spain finally lost its empire, as the strife-torn homeland could do little against the independence movements of Latin America.

When Fernando died, another war of succession broke out, this time between supporters of his brother Don Carlos and his infant daughter Isabella. The so-called Carlist Wars of 1833-1839, 1847-1849 (although this is sometimes not counted as one) and 1872-1876 were politically complex. Don Carlos represented conservatism and his support was drawn from a number of sources. Wealthy landowners, the church and the reactionary peasantry, with significant French support, lined up against the loyalist army, the liberals and the urban middle and working classes. In between and during the wars, a series of *pronunciamientos* (coups d'état) plagued the monarchy. In 1834, after Fernando's death, another, far less liberal constitution was drawn up. An important development for Andalucía took place in 1835 when the Prime Minister, desperate for funds to prosecute the war against the Carlists, confiscated church and monastery property in the Disentailment Act. The resulting sale of the vast estates aided nobody but the large landowners, who bought them up at bargain prices, further skewing the distribution of arable land in Andalucía towards the wealthy.

Despite the grinding poverty, the middle years of the 19th century saw the beginnings of what was eventually to save Andalucía: tourism. Travellers, such as Washington Irving, Richard Ford and Prosper Merimée, came to the region and enthralled the world with tales of sighing Moorish princesses, feisty *sevillanas*, bullfights, gypsies, bandits and passion. While to the 21st-century eye, the uncritical romanticism of these accounts is evident, they captured much of the magic that contemporary visitors still find in the region and have inspired generations of travellers to investigate Spain's south.

During the third Carlist war, the king abdicated and the short-lived First Spanish Republic was proclaimed, ended by a military-led restoration a year later. The Carlists were defeated but remained strong and played a prominent part in the Spanish Civil War. (Indeed, there's still a Carlist party.) As if generations of war weren't enough, the wine industry of Andalucía received a crippling blow with the arrival of the phylloxera pest, which devastated the region.

The 1876 constitution proclaimed by the restored monarchy after the third Carlist war provided for a peaceful alternation of power between liberal and conservative parties. In the wake of decades of strikes and *pronunciamientos* this was not a bad solution and the introduction of the vote for the whole male population in 1892 offered much hope. The ongoing curse, however, was *caciquismo*, a system whereby elections and governments were hopelessly rigged by influential local groups of 'mates'.

Spain lost its last overseas possessions; Cuba, Puerto Rico and the Phillippines, in the 'Disaster' of 1898. The introspective turmoil caused by this event gave the name to the '1898 generation', a forward-thinking movement of artists, philosophers and poets among whom were numbered the poets Antonio Machado and Juan Ramón Jiménez, the philosophers José Ortega y Gasset and Miguel de Unamuno and the painter Ignacio de Zuloaga. It was a time of discontent, with regular strikes culminating in the Semana Trágica (tragic week) in Barcelona in 1909, a week of church-burning and rioting sparked by the government's decision to send a regiment of Catalan conscripts to fight in the 'dirty war' in Morocco; the revolt was then brutally suppressed by the army. The growing disaffectation of farmworkers in Andalucía, forced for centuries into seasonal labour on the vast *latifundias* with no security and minimal earnings, led to a strong anarchist movement in the region. The CNT, the most prominent of the 20th-century anarchist confederations, was founded in Sevilla in 1910.

The Second Republic

The early years of the 20th century saw repeated changes of government under King Alfonso XIII. A massive defeat in Morocco in 1921 increased the discontent with the monarch, but General Miguel Primo de Rivera, a native of Jerez de la Frontera, led a coup and installed himself as dictator under Alfonso in 1923. One of his projects was the grandiose Ibero-American exhibition in Sevilla. The preparation for this lavish event effectively created the modern city we know today and, despite bankrupting the city, set the framework for a 20th-century urban centre.

Primo de Rivera's rule was relatively benign, but growing discontent eventually forced the king to dismiss him. Having broken his coronation oath to uphold the constitution, Alfonso himself was soon toppled as republicanism swept the country. The anti-royalists achieved excellent results in elections in 1931 and the king drove to Cartagena and took a boat out of the country to exile. The Second Republic was joyfully proclaimed by the left.

Things moved quickly in the short period of the republic. The new leftist government moved fast to drastically reduce the church's power. The haste was ill-advised and triumphalist and served to severely antagonize the conservatives and the military. The granting of home rule to Catalunya was even more of a blow to the establishment and their belief in Spain as an indissoluble *patria*, or fatherland.

Through this period, there was increasing anarchist activity in Andalucía, where land was seized as a reaction to the archaic *latifundia* system under which prospects for the workers, who were virtually serfs, were nil. Anarchist cooperatives were formed to share labour and produce in many of the region's rural areas. Squabbling among leftist factions contributed to the government's lack of control of the country, which propelled the right to substantial gains in elections in 1933. Government was eventually formed by a centrist coalition, with the right powerful enough to heavily influence lawmaking. The 1933 elections also saw José Antonio Primo de Rivera, son of the old dictator, elected to a seat on a fascist platform. Although an idealist and no man of violence, he founded the Falange, a group of fascist youth that became an increasingly powerful force and one which was responsible for some of the most brutal deeds before, during and immediately after the Spanish Civil War.

The new government set about reversing the reforms of its predecessors; provocative and illegal infractions of labour laws by employers didn't help the workers' moods. Independence rumblings in Catalunya and the Basque country began to gather momentum, but it was in Asturias that the major confrontation took place. The left, mainly consisting of armed miners, seized the civil buildings of the province and the government response was harsh, with generals Goded and Franco embarking on a brutal spree of retribution with their well-trained Moroccan troops.

The left was outraged and the right feared complete revolution; the centre ceased to exist, as citizens and politicians were forced to one side or the other. The elections of February 1936 were very close, but the left unexpectedly defeated the right. In an increasingly violent climate, mobilized Socialist youth and the Falange were clashing daily, while land seizures continued. A group of generals began to plan a coup and in July 1936 a military conspiracy saw garrisons throughout Spain rise against the government and try to seize control of their provinces and towns. Within a few days, battle lines were clearly drawn between the Republicans (government) and the Nationalists, a coalition of military, Carlists, fascists and the Christian right. Most of northern Spain rapidly went under Nationalist control, while Madrid remained Republican. In Andalucía, Córdoba, Cádiz, Sevilla, Huelva and Granada were taken by Nationalists, but the remainder was in loyalist hands.

In the immediate aftermath of the uprising, frightening numbers of civilians were shot behind the lines, including the Granadan poet, Federico García Lorca. This brutality continued throughout the war, with chilling atrocities committed on both sides.

The most crucial blow of the war was struck early. Francisco Franco, one of the army's best generals, had been posted to the Canary Islands by the government, who were rightly fearful of coup attempts. As the uprising occurred, Franco was flown to Morocco where he took command of the crack North African legions. The difficulty was crossing into Spain: this was achieved in August in an airlift across the Straits of Gibraltar by German planes. Franco swiftly advanced through Andalucía where his battle-hardened troops met with little resistance. Meanwhile, the other main battle lines were north of Madrid and in Aragón, where the Republicans made a determined early push for Zaragoza.

At a meeting of the revolutionary generals in October 1936, Franco had himself declared *generalísimo*, the supreme commander of the Nationalists. Few could have suspected that he would rule the nation for nearly four decades. Although he had conquered swathes of Andalucía and Extremadura with little difficulty, the war wasn't to be as short as it might have appeared. Advancing on Madrid, he detoured to relieve the besieged garrison at Toledo; by the time he turned his attention back to the capital, the defences had been shored up and Madrid resisted throughout the war.

A key aspect of the Spanish Civil War was international involvement. Fascist Germany and Italy had troops to test, and a range of weaponry to play with; these countries gave massive aid to the Nationalist cause as a rehearsal for the Second World War, which was appearing increasingly inevitable. Russia provided the Republicans with some material, but inscrutable Stalin never committed his full support. Other countries, such as Britain, USA and France, disgracefully maintained a charade of international non-intervention despite the flagrant breaches by the above nations. Notwithstanding, thousands of volunteers mobilized to form the international brigades to help out the Republicans. Enlisting for idealistic reasons to combat the rise of fascism, many of these soldiers were writers and poets such as George Orwell and WH Auden.

Although Republican territory was split geographically, far more damage was done to their cause by ongoing and bitter infighting between anarchists, socialists, Soviet-backed communists and independent communists. There was constant struggling for power, political manoeuvring, backstabbing and outright violence, which the well-organized Nationalists must have watched with glee. The climax came in Barcelona in May 1937, when the Communist party took up arms against the anarchists and the POUM, an independent communist group. The city declined into a mini civil war of its own until order was restored. Morale, however, had taken a fatal blow.

Cities continued to fall to the Nationalists, for whom the German Condor legion proved a decisive force. In the south, the armies were under the command of Gonzalo Queipo de Llano, who though of broadly republican sympathies, was one of the original conspirators, and had expertly taken Sevilla at the beginning of things. Although his propaganda broadcasts throughout the war revealed him to be a kind of psychopathic humourist, this charismatic aristocrat was an impressive general and took Málaga in early 1937. Fleeing refugees were massacred by tanks and aircraft. Republican hopes now rested solely in the outbreak of a Europe-wide war. Franco had set up base appropriately in deeply conservative Burgos; Nationalist territory was the venue for many brutal reprisals against civilians perceived as leftist, unionist, democratic, or owning a tasty little piece of land on the edge of the village. Republican atrocities in many areas were equally appalling although rarely sanctioned or perpetrated by the government.

The Republicans made a couple of last-ditch efforts in early 1938 at Teruel and in the Ebro valley but were beaten in some of the most gruelling fighting of the Civil War. The Nationalists reached the Mediterranean, dividing Catalunya from the rest of Republican territory and, after the ill-fated Republican offensive over the Ebro, putting Barcelona under intense pressure; it finally fell in January 1939. Even at this late stage, given united resistance, the Republicans could have held out a while longer and the World War might have prevented a Franco victory, but it wasn't to be. The fighting spirit had largely dissipated and the infighting led to meek capitulation. Franco entered Madrid and the war was declared over on 1 April 1939.

If Republicans were hoping that this would signal the end of the slaughter and bloodshed, they didn't know the *generalísimo* well enough. A vengeful spate of executions, lynchings, imprisonments and torture ensued and the dull weight of the new regime stifled growth and optimism. Although many thousands of Spaniards fought in the Second World War (on both sides), Spain remained nominally neutral. After meeting Franco at Hendaye, Hitler declared that he would prefer to have three or four teeth removed than have to do so again. Franco had his eye on French Morocco and was hoping to be granted it for minimal Spanish involvement; Hitler accurately realized that the country had little more to give in the way of war effort and didn't offer an alliance.

The post-war years were tough in Spain, particularly in poverty-stricken Andalucía, where the old system was back in place and the workers penniless. Franco was an international outcast and the 1940s and 1950s were bleak times. Thousands of Andalucíans left in search of employment and a better life in Europe, the USA and Latin America. The Cold War was to prove Spain's saviour. Franco was nothing if not anti-communist and the USA began to see his potential as an ally.

Eisenhower offered to provide a massive aid package in exchange for Spanish support against the Eastern Bloc. In practice, this meant the creation of American airbases on Spanish soil; one of the biggest is at Rota, just outside Cádiz.

The dollars were dirty, but the country made the most of them; Spain boomed in the 1960s as industry finally took off and the flood of tourism to the Andalucían coasts began in earnest. But dictatorship was no longer fashionable in western Europe and Spain was regarded as a slightly embarassing cousin. It was not invited to join the European Economic Community (EEC) and it seemed as if nothing was going to really change until Franco died. He finally did, in 1975, and his appointed successor, King Juan Carlos I, the grandson of Alfonso XIII, took the throne of a country burning with democratic desires.

La Transición

The king was initially predicted to be just a pet of Franco's and therefore committed to maintaining the stultifying status quo, but he surprised everyone by acting swiftly to appoint the young Adolfo Suárez as prime minister. Suárez bullied the parliament into approving a new parliamentary system; political parties were legalized in 1977 and elections held in June that year. The return to democracy was known as *la transición*; the accompanying cultural explosion became known as *la movida (madrileña)*. Suárez's centrist party triumphed and he continued his reforms. The 1978 constitution declared Spain a parliamentary monarchy with no official religion; Franco must have turned in his grave and Suárez faced increasing opposition from the conservative elements in his own party. He resigned in 1981 and as his successor was preparing to take power, the good old Spanish tradition of the *pronunciamiento* came to the fore once again. A detachment of *Guardia Civil* stormed parliament in their comedy hats and Lieutenant Colonel Tejero, pistol waving and moustache twitching, demanded everyone hit the floor. After a tense few hours in which it seemed that the army might come out in support of Tejero, the king remained calm and, dressed in his capacity as head of the armed forces, assured the people of his commitment to democracy. The coup attempt thus failed and Juan Carlos was seen in an even better light.

In 1982, the Socialist government (PSOE) of Felipe González was elected. Hailing from Sevilla, he was committed to improving conditions and infrastructure in his native Andalucía. The single most important legislation since the return to democracy was the creation of the *comunidades autónomas*, in which the regions of Spain were given their own parliaments, which operate with varying degrees of freedom from the central government. This came to bear in 1983, although it was a process initiated by Suárez. Sevilla became the capital of the Andalucían region.

The Socialists held power for 14 years and oversaw Spain's entry into the EEC (now EU) in 1986, from which it has benefited immeasurably, although rural Andalucía remains poor by western European standards. But mutterings of several scandals began to plague the PSOE government and González was really disgraced when he was implicated in having commissioned death squads with the aim of terrorizing the Basques into renouncing terrorism, which few of them supported in any case.

Culture

Architecture

Spain's architectural heritage is one of Europe's richest and certainly its most diverse, due in large part to the dual influences of European Christian and Islamic styles during the eight centuries of Moorish presence in the peninsula. Another factor is economic: both during the *Reconquista* and in the wake of the discovery of the Americas, money seemed limitless and vast building projects were undertaken. Entire treasure fleets were spent in erecting lavish churches and monasteries on previously Muslim soil, while the relationships with Islamic civilization spawned some fascinating styles unique to Spain. The Moors adorned their towns with sensuous palaces, such as Granada's Alhambra, and elegant mosques, as well as employing compact climate-driven urban planning that still forms the hearts of most towns. In modern times Spain has shaken off the ponderous monumentalism of the Franco era and become something of a powerhouse of modern architecture.

Andalucía's finest early stone structures are in Antequera, whose dolmens are extraordinarily monumental burial spaces built from vast slabs of stone. The dwellings of the period were less permanent structures of which little evidence remains, except at the remarkable site of **Los Millares** near Almería, a large Chalcolithic settlement, necropolis, and sophisticated associated fortifications that has provided valuable information about society in the third millennium BC. The first millennium BC saw the construction of further fortified settlements, usually on hilltops. Little remains of this period in Andalucía, as the towns were then occupied by the Romans and Moors.

Similarly, while the Phoenicians established many towns in southern Spain, their remains are few; they were so adept at spotting natural harbours that nearly all have been in continual use ever since, leaving only the odd foundations or breakwater. There are also few Carthaginian remains of note. Their principal base in Andalucía was Cádiz, but two millennia of subsequent occupation have taken their toll on the archaeological record.

The story of Spanish architecture really begins with the Romans, who colonized the peninsula and imposed their culture on it to a significant degree. More significant still is the legacy they left; architectural principles that endured and to some extent formed the basis for later peninsular styles.

There's not a wealth of outstanding monuments; **Itálica**, just outside Sevilla, and **Baelo Claudia**, on the Costa de la Luz, are impressive, if not especially well-preserved Roman towns. **Acinipo**, near Ronda, has a large and spectacularly sited theatre, **Carmona** has a beautifully excavated necropolis and **Almuñécar** has the ruins of its fish sauce factory on display. In many towns and villages you can see Roman fortifications and foundations under existing structures.

There are few architectural reminders of the Visigothic period, although it was far from a time of lawless barbarism. Germanic elements were added to Roman and local traditions and there was widespread building; the kings of the period commissioned many churches, but in Andalucía these were all demolished to make way for mosques.

The first distinct period of Moorish architecture in Spain is that of the Umayyads who ruled as emirs, then as caliphs, from Córdoba from the eighth to 11th centuries. Although the Moors immediately set about building mosques, the earliest building still standing is Córdoba's **Mezquita**. Dating from the late ninth century, the ruined church at the mountain stronghold of Bobastro exhibits clear stylistic similarities with parts of the Mezquita and indicates that already a specifically *Andalusi* architecture was extant.

The period of the caliphate was the high point of Al-Andalus and some suitably sumptuous architecture remains. Having declared himself caliph, Abd al-Rahman III had the palace complex of **Madinat az-Zahra** built just outside of Córdoba. Now in ruins, excavation and reconstruction have revealed some of the one-time splendour, particularly of the throne room, which has arcades somewhat similar to those of the Mezquita and ornate relief designs depicting the Tree of Life and other vegetal motifs. The residential areas are centred around courtyards, a feature of Roman and Moorish domestic architecture that persists in Andalucía to this day.

The Mezquita had been added to by succeeding rulers, who enlarged it but didn't stray far from the original design. What is noticeable is a growing ornamentality, with use of multi-lobed arches, sometimes interlocking, and blind arcading on gateways. The *mihrab* was resituated and topped with a recessed dome, decorated with lavish mosaic work, possibly realized by Byzantine craftsmen. A less ornate mosque from this period can be seen in a beautiful hilltop setting at **Almonaster la Real** in the north of Huelva province.

Many defensive installations were also put up at this time: the castles of Tarifa and Baños de la Encina mostly date from this period. Bathhouses such as those of Jaén were also in use, although were modified in succeeding centuries. The typical Moorish *hammam* had a domed central space and vaulted chambers with star-shaped holes in the ceiling to admit natural light.

The *taifa* period, although politically chaotic, continued the rich architectural tradition of the caliphate. Málaga's **Alcazaba** preserved an 11th-century pavilion with delicate triple arches on slender columns. Elaborate stucco decoration, usually with repeating geometric or vegetal motifs, began to be used commonly during this time.

The Almoravids contributed little to Andalucían architecture, but the Almohads brought their own architectural modifications with them. Based in Sevilla, their styles were not as flamboyant and relied heavily on ornamental brickwork. The supreme example of the period is the **Giralda tower** that once belonged to the Mosque in Sevilla and now forms part of the cathedral. The use of intricate wood-panelled ceilings began to be popular and the characteristic Andalucían azulejo decorative tiles were first used at this time. Over this period the horseshoe arch developed a point. The Almohads were great military architects and built or improved a large number of walls, fortresses and towers; these often have characteristic pointed battlements. The **Torre del Oro** in Sevilla is one of the most famous and attractive examples.

The climax of Moorish architecture ironically came when Al-Andalus was already doomed and had been reduced to the emirate of Granada. Under the Nasrid rulers of that city the sublime **Alhambra** was constructed; a palace and pleasure garden that took elegance and sophistication in architecture to previously unseen levels. Nearly all the attention was focused on the interior of the buildings, which consisted of galleries and courtyards offset by water features and elegant gardens. The architectural high point of this and other buildings is the sheer intricacy of the stucco decoration in panels surrounding the windows and doorways. Another ennobling feature is *mocárabes*, a curious concave decoration of prisms placed in a cupola or ceiling and resembling natural crystal formations in caves. The Alcázar in Sevilla is also a good example of the period, though actually constructed in Christian Spain; it is very Nasrid in character and Granadan craftsmen certainly worked on it.

As the Christians gradually took back Andalucía, they introduced their own styles, developed in the north with substantial influence from France and Italy. The Romanesque barely features in Andalucía; it was the Gothic style that influenced post-Reconquista church building in the 13th, 14th and 15th centuries. It was combined with styles learned under the Moors to form an Andalucían fusion known as Gothic-*mudéjar*. Many of the region's churches are constructed on these lines, typically featuring a rectangular floor plan with a triple nave surrounded by pillars, a polygonal chancel and square chapels. Gothic exterior buttresses were used and many had a bell tower decorated with ornate brickwork reminiscent of the Giralda, which was also rebuilt during this period.

The Andalucían Gothic style differs from the rest of the peninsula in its basic principles. Whereas in the north, the 'more space, less stone, more light' philosophy pervaded, practical considerations demanded different solutions in the south. One of these was space; the cathedrals normally occupied the site of the former mosque, which had square ground plans and were hemmed in by other buildings. Another was defence – on the coast in particular, churches and cathedrals had to be ready to double as fortresses in case of attack, so sturdy walls were of more importance than stained glass. The redoubt of a cathedral at Almería is a typical example. Many of Andalucía's churches, built in the Gothic style, were heavily modified in succeeding centuries and present a blend of different architectures.

Mudéjar architecture spread quickly across Spain. Moorish architects and those who worked with them began to meld their Islamic tradition with the northern influences. The result is distinctive and pleasing, typified by the decorative use of brick and coloured tiles, with tall elegant bell towers a particular highlight. Another common feature is the highly elaborate wooden panelled ceilings, some of which are masterpieces. The word *artesonado* describes the most characteristic type of these. The style became popular nationwide; in certain areas, *mudéjar* remained a constant feature for over 500 years of building.

The final phase of Spanish Gothic was the Isabelline, or Flamboyant. Produced during and immediately after the reign of the Catholic Monarchs (hence the name), it borrowed decorative motifs from Islamic architecture to create an exuberant form characterized by highly elaborate façades carved with tendrils, sweeping curves and geometrical patterns. The Capilla Real in Granada is an example and the Palacio de Jabalquinto in Baeza is a superb demonstration of the style.

The 16th century was a high point in Spanish power and wealth, when it expanded across the Atlantic, tapping riches that must have seemed limitless. Spanish Renaissance architecture reflected this, leading from the late Gothic style into the elaborate peninsular style known as Plateresque. Although the style originally relied heavily on Italian models, it soon took on specifically Spanish features. The word refers particularly to the façades of civil and religious buildings, characterized by decoration of shields and other heraldic motifs, as well as geometric and naturalistic patterns such as shells. The term comes from the word for silversmith, *platero*, as the level of intricacy of the stonework approached that of jewellery. Arches went back to the rounded and columns and piers became a riot of foliage and 'grotesque' scenes.

A classical revival put an end to much of the elaboration, as Renaissance architects concentrated on purity. To classical Greek features such as fluted columns and pediments were added large Italianate cupolas and domes. Spanish architects were apprenticed to Italian masters and returned to Spain with their ideas. Elegant interior patios in *palacios* are an especially attractive feature of the style, to be found across the country. Andalucía is a particularly rich storehouse of this style, where the master Diego de Siloé designed numerous cathedrals and churches. The palace of Carlos V in the Alhambra grounds is often cited as one of the finest examples of Renaissance purity. One of Diego de Siloé's understudies, Andrés de Vandelvira, evolved into the über-architect of the Spanish Renaissance. The ensemble of palaces and churches he designed in Jaén province, particularly in the towns of Úbeda and Baeza, are unsurpassed in their sober beauty. Other fine 16th-century *palacios* can be found in nearly every town and city of Andalucía; often built in honey-coloured sandstone, these noble buildings were the homes of the aristocrats who had reaped the riches of the Reconquista and the new trade routes to the Americas.

The pure lines of this Renaissance classicism were soon to be transformed into a new style, Spanish Baroque. Although it started fairly soberly, it soon became rather ornamental, often being used to add elements to existing buildings. The Baroque was a time of great genius in architecture as in the other arts in Spain, as masters playfully explored the reaches of their imaginations; a strong reaction against the sober preceding style. Churches became ever larger, in part to justify the huge façades, and nobles indulged in one-upmanship, building ever-grander *palacios*. The façades themselves are typified by such features as pilasters (narrow piers descending to a point) and niches to hold statues. Andalucía has a vast array of Baroque churches; Sevilla in particular bristles with them, while Cádiz cathedral is almost wholly built in this style. Smaller towns, such as Priego de Córdoba and Écija, are also well endowed, as they both enjoyed significant agriculture-based prosperity during the period.

The Baroque became more ornate as time went on, reaching the extremes of Churrigueresque, named for the Churriguera brothers who worked in the late 17th and early 18th centuries. The result can be overelaborate but on occasion transcendentally beautiful. Vine tendrils and cherubs decorate façades and *retablos*, which seem intent on breaking every classical norm, twisting here, upside-down there and at their best seeming to capture motion.

Neoclassicism, encouraged by a new interest in the ancient civilizations of Greece and Rome, was an inevitable reaction to such *joie de vivre*. It again resorted to the cleaner lines of antiquity, which were used this time for public spaces as well as civic and religious buildings. Many plazas and town halls in Spain are in this style, which tended to flourish in the cities that were thriving in the late 18th and 19th centuries, such as Cádiz, whose elegant old town is largely in this style. The best examples use symmetry to achieve beauty and elegance, such as the Prado in Madrid, or Sevilla's tobacco factory, which bridges Baroque and neoclassical styles.

The late 19th century saw Catalan *modernista* architecture break the moulds in a startling way. At the forefront of the movement was Antoni Gaudí. Essentially a highly original interpretation of art nouveau, Gaudí's style featured naturalistic curves and contours enlivened with stylistic elements inspired by Muslim and Gothic architecture. There is little *modernista* influence in Andalucía, but more sober *fin de siècle* architecture can be seen in Almería, which was a prosperous industrial powerhouse at the time.

Awakened interest in the days of Al-Andalus led to the neo-Moorish (or neo-*mudéjar*) style being used for public buildings and private residences. The most evident example of this is the fine ensemble of buildings constructed in Sevilla for the 1929 Ibero-American exhibition. Budgets were thrown out the window and the lavish pavilions are sumptuously decorated. Similarly ornate is the theatre in Cádiz.

Elegance and whimsy never seemed to play much part in fascist architecture and during the Franco era Andalucía was subjected to an appalling series of ponderous concrete monoliths, all in the name of progress. A few avant-garde buildings managed to escape the drudgery from the 1950s on, but it was the dictator's death in 1975, followed by EEC membership in 1986, that really provided the impetus for change.

Andalucía is not at the forefront of Spain's modern architectural movements, but the World Expo in Sevilla in 1992 brought some of the big names in. Among the various innovative pavilions, Santiago Calatrava's sublime bridges stand out. The impressive Teatro de la Maestranza and public library also date from this period, while the newer Olympic stadium, and Málaga's Picasso Museum and Centro de Arte Contemporáneo – both successful adaptations of older buildings – are more recent offerings. Sevilla's fantastic Parasol building, daringly built over a square in the old town, is the latest spectacular construction. Elsewhere, the focus has been on softening the harsh Francoist lines of the cities' 20th-century expansions. In most places this has been quietly successful. Much of the coast, however, is still plagued by the concrete curse, where planning laws haven't been strict enough in some places, and have been circumvented with a well-placed bribe in others.

In the first millennium BC, Iberian cultures produced fine jewellery from gold and silver, as well as some remarkable sculpture and ceramics.These influences derived from contact with trading posts set up by the Phoenicians, who also left artistic evidence of their presence, mostly in the port cities they established. Similarly, the Romans brought their own artistic styles to the peninsula and there are many cultural remnants, including some fine sculpture and a number of elaborate mosaic floors. Later, the Visigoths were skilled artists and craftspeople and produced many fine pieces, most notably in metalwork.

The majority of the artistic heritage left by the Moors is tied up in their architecture (see below). As Islamic tradition has tended to veer away from the portrayal of human or animal figures, the norm was intricate applied decoration with calligraphic, geometric and vegetal themes predominating. Superb panelled ceilings are a feature of Almohad architecture; a particularly attractive style being that known as *artesonado*, in which the concave panels are bordered with elaborate inlay work. During this period, glazed tiles known as azulejos began to be produced; these continue to be a feature of Andalucían craftsmanship.

The gradual process of the *Reconquista* brought Christian styles into Andalucía. Generally speaking, the Gothic, which had arrived in Spain both overland from France and across the Mediterranean from Italy, was the first post-Moorish style in Andalucía. Over time, Gothic sculpture achieved greater naturalism and became more ornate, culminating in the technical mastery of sculptors and painters, such as Pedro Millán, Pieter Dancart (who is responsible for the massive altarpiece of Sevilla's cathedral) and Alejo Fernández, all of whom were from or heavily influenced by northern Europe.

Though to begin with, the finest artists were working in Northern Spain, Andalucía soon could boast several notable figures of its own. In the wake of the Christian conquest of Granada, the Catholic Monarchs and their successor Carlos V went on a building spree. The Spanish Renaissance drew heavily on the Italian but developed its own style. Perhaps the finest 16th-century figure is Pedro de Campaña, a Fleming whose exalted talent went largely unrecognized in his own time. His altarpiece of the Purification of Mary in Sevilla's cathedral is particularly outstanding. The Italian sculptor Domenico Fancelli was entrusted by Carlos to carve the tombs of Fernando and Isabel in Granada; these are screened by a fine *reja* (grille) by Maestro Bartolomé, a Jaén-born artist who has several such pieces in Andalucían churches. The best-known 16th-century Spanish artist, the Cretan Domenikos Theotokopoulos (El Greco), has a few works in Andalucía, but the majority are in Toledo and Madrid.

As the Renaissance progressed, naturalism in painting increased, leading into the Golden Age of Spanish art. As Sevilla prospered on New World riches, the city became a centre for artists, who found wealthy patrons in abundance. Pre-eminent among all was Diego Rodríguez de Silva Velázquez (1599-1660), who started his career there before moving to Madrid to become a court painter. Another remarkable painter working in Sevilla was Francisco de Zurbarán (1598-1664) whose idiosyncratic style often focuses on superbly rendered white garments in a dark, brooding background, a metaphor for the subjects themselves, who were frequently priests. During Zurbarán's later years, he was eclipsed in the Sevilla popularity stakes by Bartolomé Esteban Murillo (1618-1682). While at first glance his paintings can seem heavy on the sentimentality, they tend to focus on the space between the central characters, who interact with glances or gestures of great power and meaning. Juan Valdés Leal painted many churches and monasteries in Sevilla; his greatest works are the macabre realist paintings in the Hospital de la Caridad. The sombre tone struck by these works reflects the decline of the once-great mercantile city.

At this time, the sculptor Juan Martínez Montañés carved numerous figures, *retablos* and *pasos* (ornamental floats for religious processions) in wood. Pedro Roldán, Juan de Mesa and Pedro de Mena were other important Baroque sculptors from this period, as was Alonso Cano, a crotchety but talented painter and sculptor working from Granada. The main focus of this medium continued to be ecclesiastic; *retablos* became ever larger and more ornate, commissioned by nobles to gain favour with the church and improve their chances in the afterlife.

The 18th and early 19th centuries saw fairly characterless art produced under the new dynasty of Bourbon kings. Tapestry production increased markedly but never scaled the heights of the earlier Flemish masterpieces. One man who produced pictures for tapestries was the master of 19th-century art, Francisco Goya. Goya was a remarkable figure whose finest works included both paintings and etchings; there's a handful of his work scattered around Andalucía's galleries, but the best examples are in Madrid's Prado and in the north.

After Goya, the 19th century produced few works of note as Spain tore itself apart in a series of brutal wars and conflicts. Perhaps in reaction to this, the *costumbrista* tradition developed; these painters and writers focused on portraying Spanish life; their depictions often revolving around nostalgia and stereotypes. Among the best were the Bécquer family: José; his cousin Joaquín; and his son Valeriano, whose brother Gustavo Adolfo was one of the period's best-known poets.

The early 20th century saw the rise of Spanish modernism and surrealism, much of it driven from Catalunya. While architects such as Gaudí managed to combine their discipline with art, it was one man from Málaga who had such an influence on 20th-century painting that he is arguably the most famous artist in the world. Pablo Ruiz Picasso (1881-1973) is notable not just for his artistic genius, but also for his evolution through different styles. Training in Barcelona, but doing much of his work in Paris, his initial Blue Period was fairly sober and subdued, named for predominant use of that colour. His best early work, however, came in his succeeding Pink Period, where he used brighter tones to depict the French capital. He moved on from this to become a pioneer of cubism. Drawing on non-western forms, cubism forsook realism for a new form of three-dimensionality, trying to show subjects from as many different angles as possible. Picasso then moved on to more surrealist forms. He continued painting right throughout his lifetime and produced an incredible number of works. One of his best-known paintings is *Guernica*, a nightmarish ensemble of terror-struck animals and people that he produced in abhorrence of the Nationalist bombing of the defenceless Basque market town in April 1937. The Picasso Museum in Málaga displays a range of his works.

A completely different contemporary was the Córdoban Julio Romero de Torres, a painter who specialized in sensuous depictions of Andalucían women, usually fairly unencumbered by clothing. A more sober 20th-century painter was Daniel Vázquez Díaz, a Huelvan who adorned the walls of La Rábida monastery with murals on the life of Columbus.

The Civil War was to have a serious effect on art in Spain, as a majority of artists sided with the Republic and fled Spain with their defeat. Franco was far from an enlightened patron of the arts and his occupancy was a monotonous time. Times have changed, however, and the regional governments, including the Andalucían, are extremely supportive of local artists these days and the museums in each provincial capital usually have a good collection of modern works.

Literature

The peninsula's earliest known writers lived under the Roman occupation. Of these, two of the best known hailed from Córdoba; Seneca the Younger (3 BC-AD 65), the Stoic poet, philosopher and statesman who lived most of his life in Rome, and his nephew Lucan (AD 39-AD 65), who is known for his verse history of the wars between Caesar and Pompey, *Bellum Civile*. Both were forced to commit suicide for plotting against the emperor Nero. After the fall of Rome, one of the most remarkable of all Spain's literary figures was the bishop of Sevilla, San Isidoro, whose works were classic texts for over a millennium, see box, page 85.

In Al-Andalus a flourishing literary culture existed under the Córdoba caliphate and later. Many important works were produced by Muslim and Jewish authors; some were to have a large influence on European knowledge and thought. The writings of Ibn Rushd (Averroes; 1126-1198) were of fundamental importance, asserting that the study of philosophy was not incompatible with religion and commentating extensively on Aristotle; see box, opposite. The discovery of his works a couple of centuries on by Christian scholars led to the rediscovery of Aristotle and played a triggering role in the Renaissance. His contemporary in Córdoba, Maimonides (1135-1204) was one of the foremost Jewish writers of all time; writing on Jewish law, religion and spirituality in general and medicine, he remains an immense and much-studied figure; see box, opposite. Another important Jewish writer was the philosopher and poet Judah ha-Levi (1075-1141); although born in the north, he spent much of his time writing in Granada and Córdoba. Throughout the Moorish period, there were many chronicles, treatises and studies written by Arab authors, but poetry was the favoured form of literary expression. Well-crafted verses, often about love and frequently quite explicit, were penned by such authors as the Sevilla king Al-Mu'tamid and the Córdoban Ibn Hazm.

After the Moors, however, Andalucía didn't really produce any literature of note until the so-called Golden Age of Spanish writing, which came in the wake of the discovery of the Americas and the flourishing of trade and wealth; patronage was crucial for writers in those days. The most notable poet of the period is the Córdoban Luis de Góngora (1561-1627), whose exaggerated, affected style is

Averroes and Maimonides

Two of Córdoba's most famous sons, and scholars of immense historical significance, were born within a few years of each other in the city in the 12th century.

Ibn Rushd, better known as Averroes (1126-1198), was from a high-ranking Moorish family. An extraordinary polymath, he was a doctor, theologist, philosopher, mathematician and lawyer. He was well respected by the rulers of Córdoba until a backlash against philosophers saw him banished to Morocco and many of his texts burned. Averroes' primary thesis was that the study of philosophy was not incompatible with religion. He commentated extensively on Aristotle and the rediscovery of some of these works played a triggering role in the Christian Renaissance.

Moses Maimonides (Moses ben Maimun; 1135-1204) was born of Jewish parents in Córdoba, but moved on at a fairly young age, finishing up in Cairo. Like Averroes, he was a physician, and became an absolute authority on Jewish law, religion, and spirituality. He wrote several commentaries on the ancient Hebrew texts; such was his influence that it has been said that "Between Moses and Moses, there was no one like unto Moses". As with Averroes, he had a great influence on the development of philosophy in succeeding centuries.

deeply symbolic (and sometimes almost inaccessible). His work has been widely appreciated recently and critics tend to label him the greatest of all Spanish poets, though he still turns quite a few people off.

The extraordinary life of Miguel de Cervantes (1547-1616) marks the start of a rich period of Spanish literature. *Don Quijote* came out in serial form in 1606 and is rightly considered one of the finest novels ever written; it's certainly the widest-read Spanish work. Cervantes spent plenty of time in Andalucía and some of his *Novelas Ejemplares* are short stories set in Sevilla.

The Sevillian, Lope de Rueda (1505-1565), was in many ways Spain's first playwright. He wrote comedies and paved the way for the explosion of Spanish drama under the big three – Lope de Vega, Tirso de la Molina and Calderón de la Barca – when public theatres opened in the early 17th century.

The 18th century was not such a rich period for Andalucían or Spanish writing but in the 19th century the *costumbrista* movement (see page 107) produced several fine works, among them *La Gaviota* (the Seagull), by Fernán Caballero, who was actually a Sevilla-raised woman named Cecilia Böhl von Faber, and *Escenas Andaluzas* (Andalucían Scenes), by Serafín Estébanez Calderón. Gustavo Adolfo Bécquer died young having published a famous series of legends and just one volume of poetry, popular, yearning works about love. Pedro Antonio de Alarcón (1833-1901), who hailed from Guadix, is most famous for his work *The Three-Cornered Hat*, a light and amusing tale which draws heavily on Andalucían customs and characters; it was also made into a popular ballet.

BACKGROUND

Antonio Machado

Mi infancia son recuerdos de un patio de Sevilla, / y un huerto claro donde madura el limonero; / mi juventud, veinte años en tierras de Castilla; / mi historia, algunos casos que recordar no quiero

My childhood is memories of a patio in Sevilla, / and of a light-filled garden where the lemon tree grows / My youth, twenty years in the lands of Castilla / My story, some happenings I wish not to remember

Along with Federico García Lorca, Antonio Machado was Spain's greatest 20th-century poet. Part of the so-called Generation of '98 who struggled to re-evaluate Spain in the wake of losing its last colonial possessions in 1898, he was born in 1875 in Sevilla.

Growing up mostly in Madrid, he spent time in France and then lived and worked in Soria, in Castilla; much of his poetry is redolent of the harsh landscapes of that region. His solitude was exacerbated when his young wife Leonor died after three years of marriage. He then moved to Baeza, where he taught French in a local school. Like the poetry written in Soria, his work in Andalucía reflected his profound feelings for the landscape.

Machado was a staunch defender of the Republic and became something of a bard of the Civil War. Forced to flee with thousands of refugees as the Republic fell, he died not long after, in 1939, in a pensión in southern France. His will to live was dealt a bitter blow by the triumph of fascism, while his health had suffered badly during the trying journey.

At the end of the 19th century, Spain lost the last of its colonial possessions after revolts and a war with the USA. This event, known as the Disaster, had a profound impact on the nation and its date 1898 gave its name to a generation of writers and artists. This group sought to express what Spain was and had been and to achieve new perspectives for the 20th century. One of their number was Antonio Machado (1875-1939), one of Spain's greatest poets; see box, above.

Another excellent poet of this time was Juan Ramón Jiménez (1881-1958), from Moguer in Huelva province, who won the Nobel Prize in 1956. His best-known work is the long prose poem *Platero y Yo*, a lyrical portrait of the town and the region conducted as a conversation between the writer and his donkey. He was forced into exile by the Spanish Civil War.

The Granadan Federico García Lorca (see box, page 32) was a young poet and playwright of great ability and lyricism with a gypsy streak in his soul. His play *Bodas de Sangre* (Blood Wedding) sits among the finest Spanish drama ever written and his verse ranges from the joyous to the haunted and draws heavily on Andalucían folk traditions. Lorca was shot by fascist thugs in Granada just after the outbreak of hostilities in the Civil War; one of the most poignant of the thousands of atrocities committed in that bloody conflict.

Lorca was associated with the so-called Generation of 27, another loose grouping of artists and writers. One of their number was Rafael Alberti (1902-1999), a poet from El Puerto de Santa María and a close friend of Lorca's. Achieving recognition with his first book of poems, *Mar y Tierra*, Alberti was a Communist (who once met Stalin) and fought on the Republican side in the Civil War. He was forced into exile at the end of the war, only returning to Spain in 1978. Other Andalucían poets associated with this movement were the neo-romantic Luis Cernuda (1902-1963) and Vicente Aleixandre (1898-1984), winner of the 1977 Nobel Prize for his surrealist-influenced free verse. Both men were from Sevilla.

Although Aleixandre stayed in Spain, despite his poems being banned for a decade, the exodus and murder of the country's most talented writers was a heavy blow for literature. The greatest novelists of the Franco period, Camilo José Cela and Miguel Delibes, both hailed from the north, but in more recent times Andalucía has come to the fore again with Antonio Múñoz Molina (born 1956) from Ubeda in Jaén province. His *Ardor Guerrero* (*Warrior Lust*) is a bitter look at military service, while his highly acclaimed *Sepharad* is a collection of interwoven stories broadly about the Diaspora and Jewish Spain and set in various locations ranging from concentration camps to rural Andalucían villages. In 2013 he won the prestigious Prince of Asturias prize, Spain's top literary award.

Music and dance

Flamenco

Few things symbolize the mysteries of Andalucía like flamenco but, as with the region itself, much has been written that is over-romanticized, patronizing or just plain untrue. Like bullfighting, flamenco as we know it is a fairly young art, having basically developed in the 19th century. It is constantly evolving and there have been significant changes in its performance in the last century, which makes the search for classic flamenco a bit of a wild goose chase. Rather, the element to search for is authentic emotion and, beyond this, *duende*, an undefinable passion that carries singer and watchers away in a whirlwind of raw feeling, with a devil-may-care sneer at destiny.

Though there have been many excellent *payo* flamenco artists, its history is primarily a gypsy one. It was developed among the gypsy population in the Sevilla and Cádiz area but clearly includes elements of cultures encountered further away.

Flamenco consists of three basic components: *el cante* (the song), *el toque* (the guitar) and *el baile* (the dance). In addition, *el jaleo* provides percussion sounds through shouts, clicking fingers, clapping and footwork (and, less traditionally, castanets). Flamenco can be divided into four basic types: *tonás*, *siguiriyas*, *soleá* and *tangos*, which are characterized by their *comps* or form, rhythm and accentuation and are either *cante jondo* (emotionally deep)/*cante grande* (big) or *cante ligero* (lighter)/*cante chico* (small). Related to flamenco, but not in a pure form, are *sevillanas*, danced till you drop at Feria, and *rocieras*, which are sung on (and about) the annual *romería* pilgrimage to El Rocío.

For a foreigner, perhaps the classic image of flamenco is a woman in a theatrical dress clicking castanets. A more authentic image is of a singer and guitarist, both sitting rather disconsolately on ramshackle chairs, or perhaps on a wooden box to tap out a rhythm. The singer and the guitarist work together, sensing the mood of the other and improvising. A beat is provided by clapping of hands or tapping of feet. If there's a dancer, he or she will lock into the mood of the others and vice versa. The dancing is stop-start, frenetic: the flamenco can reach crescendoes of frightening intensity when it seems the singer will have a stroke, the dancer is about to commit murder, and the guitarist may never find it back to the world of the sane. These outbursts of passion are seen to their fullest in *cante jondo*, the deepest and saddest form of flamenco.

After going through a moribund period during the mid-20th century, flamenco was revived by such artists as Paco de Lucía, and the gaunt, heroin-addicted genius Camarón de la Isla, while the flamenco theatre of Joaquín Cortés put purists' noses firmly out of joint but achieved worldwide popularity. More recently, Diego 'El Cigala' carries on Camarón's angst-ridden tradition. Fusions of flamenco with other styles have been a feature of recent years, with the flamenco-rock of Ketama and the flamenco-chillout of Málaga-based Chambao achieving notable success. Granada's late Enrique Morente, a flamenco artist from the old school, outraged purists with his willingness to experiment with other artists and musical forms; his release Omega brought in a punk band to accompany him and featured flamenco covers of Leonard Cohen hits.

Other music

Music formed a large part of cultural life in the days of the Córdoba emirate and caliphate. The earliest known depiction of a lute comes from an ivory bottle dated around AD 968; the musician Ziryab, living in the 11th century, made many important modifications to the lute, including the addition of a fifth double-string.

Like other art forms, music enjoyed something of a golden age under the early Habsburg monarchs. It was during this period that the five-string Spanish guitar came to be developed and the emergence of a separate repertoire for this instrument.

In 1629 Lope de Vega wrote the libretto for the first Spanish opera, which was to become a popular form. A particular Spanish innovation was the *zarzuela*, a musical play with speech and dancing. It became widely popular in the 19th century and is still performed in the larger cities. Spain's contribution to opera has been very important and has produced in recent times a number of world-class singers such as Montserrat Caballé, Plácido Domingo, José Carreras and Teresa Berganza.

The Cádiz-born Manuel de Falla is the greatest figure in the history of a country that has produced few classical composers. He drew heavily on Andalucían themes and culture and also helped keep flamenco traditions alive.

De Falla's friendship with Debussy in Paris led to the latter's work *Ibéria*, which, although the Frenchman never visited Spain, was described by Lorca as very evocative of Andalucía. It was the latest of many Andalucía-inspired compositions, which include Bizet's *Carmen*, from the story by Prosper Merimée and Rossini's *The Barber of Seville*, based on the play by Beaumarchais.

Religion

The history of Spain and the history of the Spanish Catholic church are barely separable but, in 1978, Article 16 of the new constitution declared that Spain was now a nation without an official religion, less than a decade after Franco's right hand man, Admiral Luis Carrero Blanco, had declared that "Spain is Catholic or she is nothing".

From the sixth-century writings of San Isidoro (see box, page 85) onwards, the destiny of Spain was a specifically Catholic one. The *Reconquista* was a territorial war inspired by holy zeal, Jews and Moors were expelled in the quest for pure Catholic blood, the Inquisition demonstrated the young nation's religious insecurities and paranoias and Felipe II bled Spain dry pursuing futile wars in a vain attempt to protect his beloved Church from the spread of Protestantism. Much of the strife of the 1800s was caused by groups attempting to end or defend the power of the church, while in the 20th century the fall of the Second Republic and the Civil War was engendered to a large extent by the provocatively anticlerical actions of the leftists.

Faced with a census form, a massive 94% of Spaniards claim to be Catholics, but less than a third of them cut regular figures in the parish church. Although regular churchgoing is increasingly confined to an aged (mostly female) segment of society and seminaries struggle to produce enough priests to stock churches, it's not the whole picture. *Romerías* (religious processions to rural chapels and sites) and religious fiestas are well attended – the most famous being the boisterous Whitsun journey to El Rocío and places of pilgrimage, usually chapels housing venerated statues of the Virgin, are flooded with Spanish visitors during the summer months. Very few weddings are conducted away from the church's bosom and, come Easter, a big percentage of the male population of some towns participates in solemn processions of religious *cofradías* (brotherhoods), most famously in Sevilla. Nevertheless, the church plays an increasingly minor role in most Spaniards' lives, especially those of those born after the return to democracy.

Practicalities
Granada

Getting there

Air

There are numerous options for reaching Granada. Nearby airports in the region (Málaga, Almería and Granada) are served regularly by flights from a wide variety of European cities.

Charter flights are cheaper and are run by package holiday firms. You can find bargains through travel agencies or online. The drawback of these flights is that they usually have a fixed return flight, often only a week or a fortnight later, and they frequently depart at antisocial hours. An upside is that charter flights operate from many regional airports.

Before booking, it's worth doing a bit of online research. Three of the best search engines for flight comparisons are www.opodo.com, www.skyscanner.com and www.kayak.com, which compare prices from a range of agencies. To keep up to date with the ever-changing routes available, sites like www.flightmapper.net are handy. Flightchecker (http://flightchecker.moneysavingexpert.com) is handy for checking multiple dates for budget airline deals.

Flights from the UK

Competition has benefited travellers in recent years. Budget operators have taken a significant slice of the market and forced other airlines to compete.

Budget There are numerous budget connections from the UK to Málaga. **Easyjet** and **Ryanair** connect Andalucía – particularly Málaga – with over a dozen UK airports, while other budget airlines running various routes from the UK to Andalucía include **Flybe, Vueling, Norwegian, Jet2, Thomson** and **Monarch**. Apart from Málaga, there are lots of flights to Almería and several to Granada.

Charter There are numerous charter flights to Málaga (and some to Almería) from many British and Irish airports. **Avro** ⓘ www.avro.co.uk, **Thomas Cook** ⓘ www.thomascook.com, and **Thomson** ⓘ www.thomson.co.uk, are some of the best charter flight providers, but it's also worth checking the travel pages of newspapers for cheap deals. The website www.flightsdirect.com is also a good tool to search for charter flights.

Non-budget flights Málaga again has the most scheduled flights, with several airlines including **Iberia** and **British Airways** flying direct from London airports and a few other UK cities. From London, there are daily direct flights to Granada with **Iberia/BA** and connections via Madrid and Barcelona to several other Andalucian airports.

TRAVEL TIP

Packing for Granada

Spain is a modern European country, and you can buy almost everything you'll need here; packing light is the way to go. Remember that it can get distinctly chilly outside of summer in Granada. A GPS device is handy for navigating and a European adaptor (plug a double adaptor into it) is a must for recharging electrical goods (see page 128).

Flights from the rest of Europe

There are numerous budget airlines operating from European and Spanish cities to Málaga and Almería.

Numerous charter flights operate to Málaga and some to Almería from Germany, Scandinavia, France, the Netherlands and Belgium.

There are non-stop flights to Málaga with non-budget airlines from many major European cities.

Flights from North America and Canada

Delta fly direct from New York to Málaga, while there are fortnightly charter flights from Montreal and Toronto with **Air Transat**. Otherwise, you'll have to connect via Madrid, Barcelona, Lisbon, London or another European city to Andalucían airports. Although sometimes you'll pay little extra to Andalucía than the Madrid flight, you can often save considerably by flying to Madrid and getting the bus down south or book a domestic connection on the local no-frills airline **Vueling** ⓘ *www.vueling.com*, or **Ryanair** ⓘ *www.ryanair.com*.

Flights from Australia and New Zealand

There are no direct flights to Spain from Australia or New Zealand; the cheapest and quickest way is to connect via Frankfurt, Paris or London. It might turn out cheaper to book the Europe–Spain leg separately via a budget operator.

Road

Bus

Eurolines ⓘ *T01582-404511, www.eurolines.com*, runs several buses from major European cities to Granada, but you won't get there cheaper than a flight.

Car and sea

It's a long haul to Granada by road if you're not already in the peninsula. From the UK, you have two options if you want to take the car: take a ferry to northern Spain (www.brittany-ferries.co.uk), or cross the Channel to France and then drive down. The former option is much more expensive; it would usually work out far cheaper to fly to Granada and hire a car once you get there. For competitive fares by sea to France and Spain, check with **Ferrysavers** ⓘ *www.ferrysavers.com*, or **Direct Ferries** ⓘ *www.directferries.com*.

Granada is about 2000 km from London by road; a dedicated drive will get you there in 20-24 driving hours. By far the fastest route is to head down the west coast of France and to Burgos via San Sebastián. From here, head south via Madríd.

Train

Unless you've got a rail pass, love train travel or aren't too keen on planes, forget about getting to Granada by train from anywhere further than France; you'll save no money over the plane fare and use up days of time better spent in tapas bars. You'll have to connect via either Barcelona or Madrid. Getting to Madrid/Barcelona from London takes about a day using **Eurostar** ⓘ *www.eurostar.com, £100-250 return to Paris, and another €130 or more return to reach Madrid/Barcelona from there*. Using the train/Channel ferry combination will more or less halve the cost and double the time to Paris.

If you are planning the train journey, **Voyages-SNCF** ⓘ *www.voyages-sncf.com*, is a useful company. **RENFE**, Spain's rail network, has online timetables at www.renfe.com. Best of all is the extremely useful www.seat61.com.

Getting around

Road

Bus

Buses are the staple of Spanish public transport. When buying a ticket, always check how long the journey will take, as the odd bus will be an 'all stations to' job, calling in at villages that seem surprised to even see it.

Granada city has a single terminal, the *estación de autobuses*. Buy your tickets at the relevant window; if there isn't one, buy it from the driver. Superior classes may cost up to 60% more but offer lounge access and onboard service. Newer buses in all classes may offer Wi-Fi, personal entertainment system and sockets. Most tickets will have an *asiento* (seat number) on them; ask when buying the ticket if you prefer a *ventana* (window) or *pasillo* (aisle) seat. Some of the companies allow booking online or by phone. If you're travelling at busy times (particularly a fiesta or national holiday) always book the bus ticket in advance.

Rural bus services are slower, less frequent and more difficult to coordinate.

All bus services are reduced on Sundays and, to a lesser extent, on Saturdays; some services don't run at all on weekends.

Car

Roads and motorways The roads in Granada are good, excellent in many parts. While driving isn't as sedate as in parts of northern Europe, it's generally pretty good and you'll have few problems.

There are two types of motorway in Spain, *autovías* and *autopistas*; for drivers, they are little different. They are signposted in blue and may have tolls payable, in which case there'll be a red warning circle on the blue sign when you're entering the motorway. Tolls are generally reasonable; the quality of motorway is generally excellent. The speed limit on motorways is 120 kph, though it is scheduled to rise to 130 kph on some stretches.

Rutas Nacionales form the backbone of the country's road network. Centrally administered, they vary wildly in quality. Typically, they are choked with traffic backed up behind trucks, and there are few stretches of dual carriageway. Driving at siesta time is a good idea if you're going to be on a busy stretch. *Rutas Nacionales* are marked with a red N followed by a number. The speed limit is 100 kph outside built-up areas, as it is for secondary roads, which are usually marked with an A (Andalucía), or C (*comarcal*, or local) prefix.

In urban areas, the speed limit is 50 kph. City driving can be confusing, with signposting generally poor and traffic heavy; it's worth using a Satnav or printing off the directions that your hotel may send you with a reservation. In some towns and cities, many of the hotels are officially signposted, making things easier. Larger cities may have their historic quarter blocked off by barriers; if your hotel lies within these, ring the buzzer and say the name of the hotel, and the barriers will open. Other cities enforce restrictions by camera, so you'll have to give your number plate details to the hotel so they can register it.

Police are increasingly enforcing speed limits in Spain, and foreign drivers are liable to a large on-the-spot fine. Drivers can also be punished for not carrying two red warning triangles to place on the road in case of breakdown, a bulb-replacement kit and a fluorescent green waistcoat to wear if you break down by the side of the road. Drink driving is being cracked down on; the limit is 0.5 g/l of blood, a little lower than the equivalent in the UK, for example.

Parking Parking is a problem in nearly every town and city in Andalucía. Red or yellow lines on the side of the street mean no parking. Blue or white lines mean that some restrictions are in place; a sign will indicate what these are (typically it means that the parking is metered). Parking meters can usually only be dosed up for a maximum of two hours, but they take a siesta at lunchtime too. Print the ticket off and display it in the car. If you overstay and get fined, you can pay it off for minimal cost at the machine if you do it within an hour of the fine being issued. Parking fines are never pursued for foreign vehicles, but if it's a hire car you'll likely be liable for it. Underground car parks are common, but pricey; €15-20 a day is normal. The website www.parkopedia.es is useful for locating underground car parks and comparing their rates.

Documentation To drive in Spain, you'll need a full driving licence from your home country. This applies to virtually all foreign nationals but, in practice, if you're from an 'unusual' country, consider an International Driving Licence or official translation of your licence into Spanish.

Liability insurance is required for every car driven in Spain and you must carry proof of it. If bringing your own car, check carefully with your insurers that you're covered and get a certificate (green card).

Car hire Hiring a car is easy and cheap. The major multinationals have offices at all large towns and airports. Prices start at around €150 per week for a small car with unlimited mileage. You'll need a credit card and most agencies will either not accept under-25s or demand a surcharge. By far the cheapest place to hire a car is Málaga, where even at the airport there are competitive rates. With the bigger companies, it's always cheaper to book over the internet. The best way to look for a deal is using a price-comparison website like www.kayak.com. Drop-offs in other cities, which used to be ridiculously punitive, are now often much more affordable.

There are often hidden charges, the most common being compulsory purchase of a tank of petrol at an overpriced rate. You then have to return the car with the tank empty.

Cycling and motorcycling

Motorcycling is a good way to enjoy Granada and there are few difficulties to trouble the biker; bike shops and mechanics are relatively common. There are comparatively few outlets for motorcycle hire.

Cycling presents a curious contrast; Spaniards are mad for the competitive sport, but essentially disinterested in cycling as a means of transport, though local governments are trying to encourage it with new bike lanes and free borrowable bikes in cities. Thus there are plenty of cycling shops but few cycle-friendly features on the roads. Taking your own bike to Granada is well worth the effort as most airlines are happy to accept them, providing they come within your baggage allowance. Bikes can be taken on the train, but have to travel in the guard's van and must be registered.

Hitchhiking
Hitchhiking is fairly easy in Spain, although not much practised. The police aren't too keen on it, but with sensible placement and a clearly written sign, you'll usually get a lift without a problem, particularly in rural areas, where, in the absence of bus services, it's a more common way for locals to get about.

Taxi and bus
Granada city and the province's towns have their sights closely packed into the centre, so you won't find local buses particularly necessary. There's a fairly comprehensive network in most towns, though; the travel text indicates where they come in handy. Taxis are a good option; the minimum charge is around €2.50 in most places (it increases slightly at night and on Sundays). A taxi is available if its green light is lit; hail one on the street, call, or ask for the nearest *parada de taxis* (rank). If you're using a cab to get to somewhere beyond the city limits, there are fixed tariffs.

Train

The Spanish national rail network, **RENFE** ⓘ *T902-240202 (English-speaking operators), www.renfe.com for timetables and tickets*, is, thanks to its growing network of high-speed trains, a useful option. But generally you'll find the bus is often quicker and cheaper.

Prices vary significantly according to the type of service you are using. The standard high-speed intercity service is called *Talgo*, while other intercity services are labelled *Altaria*, *Intercity*, *Diurno* and *Estrella* (overnight). Slower local trains are called *regionales*. Alvia is a mixed AVE-Talgo service.

It's always worth buying a ticket in advance for long-distance travel, as trains are often full. The best option is to buy them via the website, which sometimes offers advance purchase discounts. The website is notoriously unreliable, with not all services appearing, and a clunky mechanism for finding connections. You can print out the ticket yourself, or print it at a railway station using the reservation code. If buying your ticket at the station, allow plenty of time for queuing. Ticket windows are labelled *venta anticipada* (in advance) and *venta inmediata* (six hours or less before the journey).

All Spanish trains are non-smoking. The faster trains will have a first-class (*preferente*) and second-class sections as well as a cafeteria. First class costs about

30% more than standard and can be a worthwhile deal on a crowded long journey. Families and groups can take advantage of the cheap 'mesa' tickets, where you reserve four seats around a table. Buying a return ticket is 10% to 20% cheaper than two singles, but you qualify for this discount even if you buy the return leg later (but not on every service).

An **ISIC student card** or **youth card** grants a discount of 20% to 25% on train services. If you're using a European railpass, be aware that you'll still have to make a reservation on Spanish trains and pay the small reservation fee (which covers your insurance). If you have turned 60, it's worth paying €6 for a Tarjeta Dorada, a seniors' card that gets you a discount of 40% on trains from Monday to Thursday, and 25% at other times.

Maps

A useful website for route planning is www.guiarepsol.com. Car hire companies have Satnavs available, though they cost a hefty supplement.

Where to stay

from *casas rurales* to campsites

The standard of accommodation in Granada is very high; even the most modest of *pensiones* is usually very clean and respectable. At time of writing, for Spain the website www.booking.com is by far the most comprehensive. If you're booking accommodation not listed in this guide, always be sure to check the location if that's important to you – it's easy to find yourself a 15-minute cab ride from the town you think you're going to be in.

Environmental issues are an individual's responsibility, and the type of holiday you choose has a direct impact on the future of the region. Opting for more sustainable tourism choices – picking a *casa rural* in a traditional village and eating in restaurants serving locally sourced food rather than staying in the four-star multinational hotel – has a small but significant knock-on effect. Don't be afraid to ask questions about environmental policy before making a hotel or *casa rural* booking.

Types of accommodation

Alojamientos (places to stay), are divided into two main categories; the distinctions between them are in an arcane series of regulations devised by the government.

Hotels, hostales and pensiones

Hoteles (marked H or HR) are graded from one to five stars and occupy their own building, which distinguishes them from many *hostales* (Hs or HsR), which go from one to two stars. The *hostal* category includes *pensiones*, the standard budget option, typically family-run and occupying a floor of an apartment building. The standard for the price paid is normally excellent, and they're nearly all spotless. Spanish traditions of hospitality are alive and well; check-out time is almost uniformly a very civilized midday.

A great number of Spanish hotels are well equipped but characterless chain business places (big players include **NH** ⓘ *www.nh-hoteles.es*, **Husa** ⓘ *www. husa.es*, **AC/Marriott** ⓘ *www.marriott.com*, **Tryp/SolMelia** ⓘ *www.solmelia.com*,

---

Price codes

Where to stay	Restaurants
€€€€ over €170	€€€ over €30
€€€ €110-170	€€ €15-30
€€ €60-110	€ under €15
€ under €60	
A standard double/twin room in high season.	A two-course meal (or two average *raciones*) for one person, without drinks.

and Riu ⓘ *www.riu.com*). This guide has expressly minimized these in the listings, preferring to concentrate on more atmospheric options.

Casas rurales

An excellent option if you've got your own transport are the networks of rural houses, called *casas rurales*. Although these are under a different classification system, the standard is often as high as any country hotel. The best of them are traditional farmhouses or characterful village cottages. Some are available only to rent out whole (often for a minimum of three days), while others offer rooms on a nightly basis. Rates tend to be excellent compared to hotels. While many are listed in the text, there are huge numbers of them. Local tourist offices will have details of nearby *casas rurales*; the tourist board website www.andalucia.org lists a good selection.

Youth hostels

There's a network of *albergues* (youth hostels), which are listed at www.inturjoven. com. These are institutional and often group-booked. Funding issues mean that many now open only seasonally. Major cities have backpacker hostels with instant social life and every mod con. *Refugios* are mountain bunkhouses, which range from unstaffed sheds to cheerful hostels with a bar and restaurant.

Campsites

Most campsites are set up as well-equipped holiday villages for families; some are open only in summer. While the facilities are good, they get extremely busy in peak season. Many have cabins or bungalows available, ranging from simple huts to houses with fully equipped kitchens and bathrooms. In other areas, camping, unless specifically prohibited, is a matter of common sense. Don't camp where you're not allowed to; prohibitions are usually there for a good reason. Fire danger can be high in summer, so respect local regulations.

Prices

Price codes refer to a standard double or twin room, inclusive of VAT. The rates are generally for high season (March-May in Granada city). Occasionally, an area or town will have a short period when prices are hugely exaggerated; this is usually due to a festival.

Breakfast is often included in the price at small intimate hotels, but rarely at the grander places, who tend to charge a fortune. Normally only the more expensive hotels have parking, and they always charge for it, normally around €10-25 per day.

All registered accommodation charge a 10% value added tax; this is usually included in the price and may be waived if you pay cash. If you have any problems, a last resort is to ask for the *libro de reclamaciones* (complaints book), an official document that, like stepping on cracks in the pavement, means uncertain but definitely horrible consequences for the hotel if anything is written in it. Be aware that you must also take a copy to the local police station for the complaint to be registered.

Food & drink

In no country in the world are culture and society as intimately connected with eating and drinking as in Spain, and in Andalucía, the spiritual home of tapas, this is even more the case.

Food → *See page 140 for a glossary of food.*

Andalucían cooking is characterized by an abundance of fresh ingredients, generally consecrated with the chef's holy trinity of garlic, peppers and local olive oil.

Spaniards eat little for breakfast and, apart from hotels in touristy places, you're unlikely to find anything beyond a *tostada* (large piece of toasted bread spread with olive oil, tomato and garlic, pâté or jam) or a pastry to go with your coffee. A common breakfast or afternoon snack are *churros*, fried dough sticks typically dipped in hot chocolate.

Lunch is the main meal and is nearly always a filling affair with three courses. Most places open for lunch at about 1300, and take last orders at 1500 or 1530, although at weekends this can extend. Lunchtime is the cheapest time to eat if you opt for the ubiquitous *menú del día*, usually a set three-course meal that includes wine or soft drink, typically costing €10 to €16. Dinner and/or evening tapas time is from around 2100 to midnight. It's not much fun sitting alone in a restaurant so try and adapt to the local hours; it may feel strange dining so late, but you'll miss out on a lot of atmosphere if you don't. If a place is open for lunch at noon, or dinner at 1900, it's likely to be a tourist trap.

Types of eateries

The great joy of eating out in Granada is going for tapas. This word refers to bar food, served in saucer-sized tapa portions typically costing €1.50-3. In Granada you'll receive a free tapa with your drink. Tapas are available at lunchtime, but the classic time to eat them is in the evening. To do tapas the Andalucían way don't order more than a couple at each place, taste each others' dishes, and stand at the bar. Locals know what the specialities of each bar are; if there's a daily special, order that. Also available are *raciones*, substantial meal-sized plates of the same fare, which also come in halves, *medias raciones*. Both are good for sharing. Considering these, the distinction between restaurants and tapas bars more or less disappears, as in the latter you can usually sit down at a table to order your *raciones*, effectively turning the experience into a meal.

Other types of eateries include the *chiringuito*, a beach bar open in summer and serving drinks and fresh seafood. A *freiduría* is a takeaway specializing in fried fish, while a *marisquería* is a classier type of seafood restaurant. In rural areas, look out for *ventas*, roadside eateries that often have a long history of feeding the passing muleteers with generous, hearty and cheap portions. The more cars and trucks outside, the better it will be. In Granada city, North African-style teahouses, *teterías*, are popular.

Vegetarian food

Vegetarians in Granada won't be spoiled for choice, but at least what there is tends to be good. There are few dedicated vegetarian restaurants and many restaurants won't have a vegetarian main course on offer, although the existence of tapas, *raciones* and salads makes this less of a burden than it might be. You'll have to specify *soy vegetariano/a* (I am a vegetarian), but ask what dishes contain, as ham, fish and even chicken are often considered suitable vegetarian fare. Vegans will have a tougher time. What doesn't have meat nearly always contains cheese or egg. Better restaurants, particularly in cities, will be happy to prepare something, but otherwise stick to very simple dishes.

On the menu

Typical starters include *gazpacho* (a cold summer tomato soup flavoured with garlic, olive oil and peppers; *salmorejo* is a thicker version from Córdoba), *ensalada mixta* (mixed salad based on lettuce, tomatoes, tuna and more), or paella.

Main courses will usually be either meat or fish and are rarely served with any accompaniment beyond chips. Beef is common; the better steaks such as *solomillo* or *entrecot* are usually superbly tender. Spaniards tend to eat them fairly rare (*poco hecho*; ask for *al punto* for medium rare or *bien hecho* for well done). Pork is also widespread; *solomillo de cerdo*, *secreto*, *pluma* and *lomo* are all tasty cuts. Innards are popular: *callos* (tripe), *mollejas* (sweetbreads) and *morcilla* (black pudding) are excellent, if acquired, tastes.

Seafood is the pride of Andalucía. The region is famous for its *pescaíto frito* (fried fish) which typically consists of small fry such as whitebait in batter. Shellfish include *mejillones* (mussels), *gambas* (prawns) and *coquillas* (cockles). *Calamares* (calamari), *sepia* or *choco* (cuttlefish) and *chipirones* (small squid) are common, and you'll sometimes see *pulpo* (octopus). Among the vertebrates, *sardinas* (sardines), *dorada* (gilthead bream), *rape* (monkfish) and *pez espada* (swordfish) are all usually excellent. In the Alpujarra and other hilly areas you can enjoy freshwater *trucha* (trout).

Signature tapas dishes vary from bar to bar and from province to province, and part of the delight of Andalucía comes trying regional specialities. Ubiquitous are *jamón* (cured ham; the best, *ibérico*, comes from black-footed acorn-eating porkers that roam the woods of Huelva province and Extremadura) and *queso* (in Andalucía, usually the hard salty *manchego* from Castilla-la Mancha). *Gambas* (prawns) are usually on the tapas list; the best and priciest are from Huelva.

Desserts focus on the sweet and milky. *Flan* (a sort of crème caramel) is ubiquitous; great when *casero* (home-made), but often out of a plastic tub. *Natillas* are a similar but more liquid version, while Moorish-style pastries are also specialities of some areas.

Drink

Alcoholic drinks

In good Catholic fashion, wine is the blood of Spain. It's the standard accompaniment to meals, but also features prominently in bars. *Tinto* is red (if you just order *vino* this is what you'll get), *blanco* is white and rosé is *rosado*.

A well-regulated system of *denominaciones de origen* (DO), similar to the French *appelation d'origine contrôlée*, has lifted the quality and reputation of Spanish wines. While the daddy in terms of production and popularity is still Rioja, regions such as the Ribera del Duero, Rueda, Bierzo, Jumilla, Priorat and Valdepeñas have achieved worldwide recognition. The words *crianza*, *reserva* and *gran reserva* refer to the length and nature of the ageing process.

One of the joys of Spain, though, is the rest of the wine. Order a *menú del día* at a cheap restaurant and you'll be unceremoniously served a cheap bottle of local red. Wine snobbery can leave by the back door at this point: it may be cold, but you'll find it refreshing; it may be acidic, but once the olive-oil laden food arrives, you'll be glad of it. People add water to it if they feel like it, or *gaseosa* (lemonade) or cola (for the party drink *calimocho*).

Andalucía produces several table wines of this sort. The whites of the Condado region in eastern Huelva province and those from nearby Cádiz are simple seafood companions, while in the Alpujarra region the nut-brown *costa*, somewhere between a conventional red and a rosé, accompanies the likeably simple local fare. In the same area, Laujar de Andarax produces some tasty cheapish reds. Jaén province also has red grapes tucked between its seas of olive trees, mainly around Torreperogil near Ubeda. Bartenders throughout Andalucía tend to assume that tourists only want Rioja, so be sure to specify *vino corriente* (or *vino de la zona*) if you want to try the local stuff. As a general rule, only bars that serve food serve wine; most *pubs* and *discotecas* won't have it. Cheaper red wine is often served cold, a refreshing alternative in summer. *Tinto de verano* is a summery mix of red wine and lemonade, often with fruit added, while the stronger *sangría* adds healthy measures of sherry and sometimes spirits to the mix. The real vinous fame of the region comes, of course, from its fortified wines; sherries and others.

Beer is mostly lager, usually reasonably strong, fairly gassy, cold and good. Sweetish Cruzcampo from Sevilla is found throughout the region; other local brews include San Miguel, named after the archangel and brewed in Málaga, and Alhambra from Granada. A *caña* or *tubo* is a glass of draught beer, while just specifying *cerveza* usually gets you a bottle, otherwise known as a *botellín*. Many people order their beer *con gas* (half beer and half fizzy sweet water) or *con limón* (half lemonade, also called a *clara*).

Vermut (vermouth) is a popular pre-lunch aperitif. Many bars make their own vermouth by adding various herbs and fruits and letting it sit in barrels.

After dinner it's time for a *copa*. People relax over a whisky or a brandy, or hit the *cubatas* (mixed drinks); gin and tonic, rum and coke, whisky and coke are the most popular. Spirits are free-poured and large.

When ordering a spirit, you'll be expected to choose which brand you want; the range of, particularly, gins, is extraordinary. There's always a good selection of rum (*ron*) and blended whisky available too. *Chupitos* are short drinks often served in shot-glasses.

Non-alcoholic drinks

Zumo (fruit juice) is normally bottled; *mosto* (grape juice, really pre-fermented wine) is a popular soft drink in bars. All bars serve alcohol-free beer (*cerveza sin alcohol*). *Horchata* is a summer drink, a sort of milkshake made from tiger nuts. *Agua* (water) comes *con* (with) or *sin* (without) *gas*. The tap water is totally safe.

Café (coffee) is excellent and strong. *Solo* is black, served espresso style. Order *americano* if you want a long black, *cortado* if you want a dash of milk, or *con leche* for about half milk. *Té* (tea) is served without milk unless you ask; herbal teas (*infusiones*) are common, especially chamomile (*manzanilla*; don't confuse with the sherry of the same name) and mint (*menta poleo*).

Essentials A-Z

Accidents and emergencies

General emergencies 112.

Customs and duty free

Non-EU citizens are allowed to import 1 litre of spirits, 2 litres of wine and 200 cigarettes or 250 g of tobacco or 50 cigars. EU citizens are theoretically limited by personal use only. Gibraltar is not part of the EU economic zone, so normal duty-free limits apply.

Disabled travellers

Spain isn't the best equipped of countries in terms of disabled travel, but things are improving rapidly. By law, all new public buildings have to have full disabled access and facilities, but disabled toilets are rare elsewhere. Facilities generally are significantly better in Andalucía than in the rest of the country.

Most trains and stations are wheelchair friendly to some degree, as are many urban buses, but intercity buses are largely not accessible. **Hertz** in Málaga have a small range of cars set up with hand controls, but be sure to book them well in advance. Nearly all underground and municipal car parks have lifts and disabled spaces, as do many museums, castles, etc.

An invaluable resource for finding a bed are the regional accommodation lists, available from tourist offices and the www.andalucia.org website. Most of these include a disabled-access criterion. Many *hostales* are in buildings with ramps and lifts, but there are many that are not, and the lifts can be very small. Nearly all paradores and chain hotels are fully accessible by wheelchair, as is any accommodation built since 1995, but it's best to phone. Be sure to check details as many hotels' claims are well intentioned but not fully thought through.

While major cities are relatively straightforward, smaller towns and villages frequently have uneven footpaths, steep streets (often cobbled) and little, if any, disabled infrastructure.

Useful contacts
Confederación Nacional de Sordos de España (CNSE), www.cnse.es, has links to local associations for the deaf.
Global Access, www.globalaccessnews.com, has regular reports from disabled travellers as well as links to other sites.
ONCE, www.once.es. The blind are well catered for as a result of the efforts of ONCE, the national organization for the blind, which runs a lucrative daily lottery. It can provide information on accessible attractions for blind travellers.

Electricity

230V. A round 2-pin plug is used (European standard).

Embassies and consulates

For a list of Spanish embassies abroad, see http://embassy.goabroad.com.

Festivals and public holidays

Festivals
In Jun/Jul is the **International Festival of Music and Dance**, in Granada. One

of Andalucía's biggest cultural events is held in the Alhambra's Carlos V Palace, with classical music and ballet shows as well as flamenco. Check the dates at www.granadafestival.org. In Dec is **Encuentros Flamencos**, which features the biggest names in flamenco, with a different theme each year. For more information, see www.facebook.com/encuentrosflamencosdegranada. Even the smallest village in Granada has a fiesta and many have several. Although mostly nominally religious featuring a mass and procession or two, they also offer live music, bullfights, competitions and fireworks. A feature of many are *gigantes y cabezudos*, huge-headed papier mâché figures based on historical personages who parade the streets. In many Andalucían villages there's a *Moros y Cristianos* festival, which recreates a Reconquista battle with colourful costumes.

Most fiestas are in summer; expect some trouble finding accommodation. Details of the major town fiestas can be found in the travel text. National holidays and *puentes* (long weekends) can be difficult times to travel; it's important to reserve tickets in advance.

Public holidays
1 Jan **Año Nuevo**, New Year's Day.
6 Jan **Reyes Magos/Epifanía**, Epiphany, when Christmas presents are given.
28 Feb **Andalucía day**.
Easter **Jueves Santo, Viernes Santo, Día de Pascua** (Maundy Thu, Good Fri, Easter Sun).
1 May **Fiesta del Trabajo** (Labour Day).
24 Jun **Fiesta de San Juan** (Feast of St John and name-day of the king Juan Carlos I).
25 Jul **Día del Apostol Santiago**, Feast of St James.
15 Aug **Asunción**, Feast of the Assumption.
12 Oct **Día de la Hispanidad**, Spanish National Day (Columbus Day, Feast of the Virgin of the Pillar).
1 Nov **Todos los Santos**, All Saints' Day.
6 Dec **El Día de la Constitución Española**, Constitution Day.
8 Dec **Inmaculada Concepción**, Feast of the Immaculate Conception.
25 Dec **Navidad**, Christmas Day.

Gay and lesbian travellers

Homosexuality is legal, as is gay marriage, though it's just the sort of thing the incumbent Partido Popular would like to revoke. There are different levels of tolerance and open-mindedness towards gays and lesbians in Granada. In Granada city and on the coast (particularly in summer), there's a substantial amount of gay life, although not on a par with Barcelona or Madrid. Inland, however, it can be a different story, and a couple walking hand-in-hand will likely be greeted with incredulous stares, although rarely anything worse.

Useful contacts
COLEGA, www.colegaweb.org. A gay and lesbian association with offices in many cities.
Shangay/Shanguide, www.shangay.com, is a useful magazine with reviews, events, information and city-by-city listings for the whole country.

Useful websites
www.damron.com Subscription listings and travel info.

Health

Medical facilities in Granada are very good. However, EU citizens should make sure they have the **European Health Insurance Card** (EHIC) to prove reciprocal rights to medical care. These are available free of charge in the UK from the Department of Health (www.dh.gov.uk) or post offices.

Non-EU citizens should consider travel insurance to cover emergency and routine medical needs; be sure that it covers any sports or activities you may do. Check for reciprocal cover with your private or public health scheme first.

Water is safe to drink. The **sun** in southern Spain can be harsh, so take precautions to avoid heat exhaustion and sunburn.

Many medications that require a prescription in other countries are available over the counter at pharmacies in Spain. Pharmacists are highly trained and usually speak some English. In medium-sized towns and cities, at least one pharmacy is open 24 hrs; this is performed on a rota system (posted in the window of all pharmacies and listed in local newspapers).

No vaccinations are needed.

Insurance

Insurance is a good idea to cover you for theft. In the unlucky event of theft, you'll have to make a report at the local police station within 24 hrs and obtain a *denuncia* (report) to show your insurers. See above for health cover for EU citizens.

Internet

Cyber cafés are increasingly rare in Spain, though you'll still find them in large cities like Granada. Other places that often offer access are *locutorios* (call shops), which are common in areas with a high immigrant population. Most accommodation and an increasing number of cafés and restaurants offer Wi-Fi. Internet places tend to appear and disappear rapidly, so we have minimized listings in this guide; ask the tourist information office for the latest place to get online. Mobile phone providers offer pay-as-you-go data SIM cards and USB modems at a reasonable rate. Roaming charges within the EU are set to be abolished in late 2015, so mobile data usage will cost EU residents no more in Andalucía than it would in your home country.

Language

Everyone in Andalucía – except many of the expat population – speaks Spanish, known either as *castellano* or *español*, and it's a huge help to know some. The local accent, *andaluz*, is characterized by dropping consonants left, right and centre, thus *dos tapas* tends to be pronounced *dotapa*. Unlike in the rest of Spain, the letters 'c' and 'z' in words such as *cerveza* aren't pronounced 'th' (although in Cádiz province, perversely, they tend to pronounce 's' with that sound).

Most young people know some English, and standards are rising fast, but don't assume that people aged 40 or over know any at all. Spaniards are often shy to attempt to speak English. On the coast, high numbers of expats and tourists mean that bartenders and shopkeepers know some English. While many visitor attractions have some sort of information available in English (and to a lesser extent French and German), many don't, or have English tours only in times of high demand. Most tourist office staff will speak at least some English and there's a good range of translated information available in most places. People are used to speaking English in well-visited areas, but trying even a couple of words of Spanish is basic politeness. Small courtesies grease the wheels of everyday interaction here: greet the proprietor or waiting staff when entering a shop or bar, and say *hasta luego* when leaving. See page 136, for useful words and phrases in Spanish and page 43 for language schools in Granada city.

Money

Currency and exchange

For up-to-the-minute exchange rates visit www.xe.com.

In 2002, Spain switched to the euro, bidding farewell to the peseta. The euro (€) is divided into 100 *céntimos*. Euro notes are standard across the whole euro zone and come in denominations of 5, 10, 20, 50, 100, and the rarely seen 200 and 500. Coins have one standard face and one national face; all coins are, however, acceptable in all countries. The coins are slightly difficult to tell apart when you're not used to them. The coppers are 1, 2 and 5 cent pieces, the golds are 10, 20 and 50, and the silver/gold combinations are €1 and €2. The exchange rate was approximately €6 to 1000 pesetas or 166 pesetas to the euro. Some people still quote large amounts, like house prices, in pesetas.

ATMs and banks

The best way to get money in Spain is by plastic. ATMs are plentiful and accept all the major international debit and credit cards. The Spanish bank won't charge for the transaction, though they will charge a mark-up on the exchange rate, but beware of your own bank hitting you for a hefty fee: check with them before leaving home. Even if they do, it's likely to be a better deal than changing cash over a counter.

Banks are usually open Mon-Fri (and Sat in winter) 0830-1430 and many change foreign money (sometimes only the central branch in a town will do it). Commission rates vary widely; it's usually best to change large amounts, as there's often a minimum commission. The website www.moneysavingexpert. com has a good rundown on the most economical ways of accessing cash while travelling.

Cost of living

Prices have soared since the euro was introduced; some basics rose by 50-80% in 3 years, and hotel and restaurant prices can even seem dear by Western European standards these days. Nevertheless, Andalucía still offers value for money, and you can get by cheaply if you forgo a few luxuries. If you're travelling as a pair, staying in cheap *pensiones*, eating a set meal at lunchtime, travelling short distances by bus or train daily, and snacking on tapas in the evenings, €65 per person per day is reasonable. If you camp and grab picnic lunches from shops, you could reduce this somewhat. In a good *hostal* or cheap hotel and using a car, €150 a day and you'll not be counting pennies; €300 per day and you'll be very comfy indeed unless you're staying in 5-star accommodation.

Accommodation is usually more expensive in summer than winter, particularly on the coast, where hotels and *hostales* in seaside towns are overpriced.

Public transport is generally cheap; intercity bus services are quick and low-priced, though the new fast trains are expensive. If you're hiring a car, Málaga is the cheapest place in Andalucía. Standard unleaded petrol is around 150 cents per litre. In some places, particularly in tourist areas, you may be charged up to 20% more to sit outside a restaurant. It's also worth checking if the 10% IVA (sales tax) is included in menu prices, especially in the more expensive restaurants; it should say on the menu.

Opening hours

Business hours Mon-Fri 1000-1400, 1700-2000; Sat 1000-1400. **Banks** Mon-Fri, plus sometimes Sat in winter, 0830-1430. **Government offices** Mornings only.

Post

The Spanish post is still notoriously inefficient and slow by European standards. *Correos* (post offices) generally open Mon-Fri 0800-1300, 1700-2000; Sat 0800-1300, although main offices in large towns will stay open all day. Stamps can be bought here or at *estancos* (tobacconists).

Safety

Granada is a very safe place to travel and there's been a crackdown on tourist crime in recent years. What tourist crime there is tends to be of the opportunistic kind. Robberies from parked cars (particularly those with foreign plates) or snatch-and-run thefts from vehicles stopped at traffic lights are not unknown, and the occasional mugger operates in the citiy of Granada, so keep car doors locked when driving.

If parking in the city or a popular hiking zone, make it clear there's nothing worth robbing in a car by opening the glove compartment.

If you are unfortunate enough to be robbed, you should report the theft immediately at the nearest police station, as insurance companies will require a copy of the *denuncia* (police report).

Smoking

Smoking is widespread in Spain, but it's been banned in all enclosed public spaces (ie bars and restaurants) since 2011. There are still rooms for smokers in some hotels, but these are limited to 30% of the total rooms. Prices are standardized; you can buy cigarettes at tobacconists or at machines in cafés and bars (with a small surcharge).

Student travellers

An **International Student Identity Card** (ISIC; www.isic.org), for full-time students, is worth having in Spain. Get one at your place of study, or at many travel agencies both in and outside Spain. The cost varies from country to country, but is generally about €6-10 – a good investment, providing discounts of up to 20% on some plane fares, train tickets, museum entries, bus tickets and some accommodation. A **European Youth Card** (www.eyca.org) card gives similar discounts for anyone under 30 years of age.

Taxes

Nearly all goods and services in Spain are subject to a value-added tax (IVA). This is 10% for things like supermarket supplies, hotels and restaurant meals, but is 21%

on luxury goods such as computer equipment. IVA is normally included in the stated prices. You're technically entitled to claim it back if you're a non-EU citizen, for purchases over €90. If you're buying something pricey, make sure you get a stamped receipt clearly showing the IVA component, as well as your name and passport number; you can claim the amount back at major airports on departure. Some shops will have a form to smooth the process.

Telephone

Country code +34; **IDD Code** 00 Phone booths on the street are dwindling. Those that remain are mostly operated by **Telefónica**, and all have international direct dialling. They accept coins from €0.05 upwards and phone cards, which can be bought from *kioscos* (newspaper kiosks).

Domestic landlines have 9-digit numbers beginning with 9. Although the first 3 digits indicate the province, you have to dial the full number from wherever you are calling, including abroad. Mobile numbers start with 6.

Most foreign mobiles will work in Spain (although older North American ones won't); check with your service provider about what the call costs will be like. Roaming charges within the EU are set to be abolished from late 2015. Many mobile networks require you to call before leaving your home country to activate overseas service (roaming). If you're staying a while and have an unlocked phone, it's pretty cheap to buy a Spanish SIM card.

Time

1 hr ahead of GMT. Clocks go forward an hour in late Mar and back in late Oct with the rest of the EU.

Tipping

Tipping in Spain is far from compulsory. A 10% tip would be considered extremely generous in a restaurant; 3% to 5% is more usual. It's rare for a service charge to be added to a bill. Waiters don't expect tips but in bars and cafés people will sometimes leave small change, especially for table service. Taxi drivers don't expect a tip, but will be pleased to receive one.

Tourist information

The tourist information infrastructure in Andalucía is organized by the Junta (the regional government) and is generally excellent, with a wide range of information, often in English, German and French as well as Spanish. The website www.andalucia.org has comprehensive information and *Oficinas de turismo* (local government tourist offices) are in all the major towns, providing more specific local information. In addition, many towns run a municipal *turismo*, offering locally produced material. The tourist offices are generally open during normal office hours and in the main holiday areas normally have enthusiastic, multilingual staff. The tourist offices can provide local maps and town plans and a full list of registered accommodation. Staff are not allowed to make recommendations. If you're in a car, it's especially worth asking for a listing of *casas rurales* (rural accommodation). In villages with no *turismo* you could try asking for local information on accommodation and sights in the *ayuntamiento* (town hall). Some city tourist offices offer downloadable smartphone content.

There is a substantial amount of tourist information on the internet. Apart from the websites listed (see below), many towns and villages have their own site with information on sights, hotels and restaurants, although this may be in Spanish.

The **Spanish Tourist Board** (www. spain.info) produces a mass of information that you can obtain before you leave from their offices located in many countries abroad.

Useful websites

www.alsa.es One of the country's main bus companies with online booking.

www.andalucia.com Excellent site with comprehensive practical and background information on Andalucía, covering everything from accommodation to zoos.

www.andalucia.org The official tourist-board site, with details of even the smallest villages, accommodation and tourist offices.

www.booking.com The most useful online accommodation booker for Spain.

www.dgt.es The transport department website has up-to-date information in Spanish on road conditions throughout the country.

www.elpais.com Online edition of Spain's biggest-selling daily paper. Also in English.

www.guiarepsol.com Online route planner for Spanish roads, also available in English.

www.inm.es Site of the national metereological institute, with the day's weather and next-day forecasts.

www.inturjoven.com Details of youth hostel locations, facilities and prices.

maps.google.es Street maps of most Spanish towns and cities.

www.movelia.es Online timetables and ticketing for some bus companies.

www.paginasamarillas.es Yellow Pages.

www.paginasblancas.es White Pages.

www.parador.es Parador information, including locations, prices and photos.

www.raar.es Andalucían rural accommodation network with details of mainly self-catering accommodation to rent, including cottages and farmhouses.

www.renfe.com Online timetables and tickets for RENFE train network.

www.spain.info The official website of the Spanish tourist board.

www.soccer-spain.com A website in English dedicated to Spanish football.

www.ticketmaster.es Spain's biggest ticketing agency for concerts and more, with online purchase.

www.toprural.com and **www.todo turismorural.com** 2 of many sites for *casas rurales*.

www.tourspain.es A useful website run by the Spanish tourist board.

www.typicallyspanish.com News and links on all things Spanish.

UK and Ireland

Abercrombie and Kent, www. abercrombiekent.com. Upmarket operator offering tailor-made itineraries in Andalucía as well as the rest of Spain.

ACE Cultural Tours, www.acecultural tours.co.uk. Trips focusing on Moorish culture, as well as wildlife.

Andante Travels, www.andantetravels. com. Popular operator running a variety of different cultural and active holidays in Andalucía. They focus on archaeology and the Roman presence.

Cycling Safaris, www.cyclingsafaris.com. Irish operator offering well-priced tours to Andalucía.

Exodus, www.exodus.co.uk. Walking and adventure tours to suit all pockets.

Iberocycle, www.iberocycle.com. Recommended bike tours, guided or self-guided, of Moorish heritage and the white towns.

In the Saddle, www.inthesaddle.com. Runs riding trips in the Sierra Nevada/Alpujarra regions.

Martin Randall Travel, www.martinrandall.com. Excellent cultural itineraries accompanied by lectures. Covers all the main cities, and also has an off-beat tour visiting some out-of-the-way spots.

Step in Time Tours, www.stepintimetours.com. Tours that focus on Moorish culture and Granada. Inclusive ethos.

Rest of Europe

Bootlace Walking Holidays, www.bootlace.com. Down-to-earth Alpujarran walking trips with vegetarian food.

Bravo Bike Travel, www.bravobike.com. Runs 8-day bike tours of Andalucía.

Las Chimeneas, www.alpujarra-tours.com. Based in Mairena in the Alpujarra region, organize packages including sweet village accommodation and self-guided hikes as well as other activities.

North America

Cycling Through The Centuries, www.cycling-centuries.com. Runs guided cycling tours of Andalucía.

Epiculinary Tours, www.epiculinary.com. Tours to delight foodies, with lessons on making tapas and other Andalucían food interspersed with plenty of tastings and cultural visits.

Heritage Tours, www.htprivatetravel.com. Interesting, classy itineraries around the south of Spain.

Magical Spain, www.magicalspain.com. American-run tour agency based in Sevilla, who run a variety of tours.

Spain Adventures, www.spainadventures.com. Organizes a range of hiking and biking tours.

Australia

Ibertours,www.ibertours.com.au. Spanish specialist and booking agent for **Parador** and **Rusticae** hotels.

Timeless Tours & Travel, www.timeless.com.au. Specializes in tailored itineraries for Spain.

Visas and immigration

EU citizens and those from countries within the Schengen agreement can enter Spain freely. UK and Irish citizens will need to carry a passport, while an identity card suffices for other EU/Schengen nationals. Citizens of Australia, the USA, Canada, New Zealand, several Latin American countries and Israel can enter without a visa for up to 90 days. Other citizens will require a visa, obtainable from Spanish consulates or embassies. These are usually issued quickly and are valid for all Schengen countries. The basic visa is valid for 90 days, and you'll need 2 passport photos, proof of funds covering your stay, and possibly evidence of medical cover (ie insurance).

For extensions of visas, apply to an *oficina de extranjeros* in a major city (usually in the *comisaría*, main police station).

Weights and measures

Metric.

Basic Spanish

Learning Spanish is a useful part of the preparation for a trip to Spain and no volumes of dictionaries, phrase books or word lists will provide the same enjoyment as being able to communicate directly with the people of the country you are visiting. It is a good idea to make an effort to grasp the basics before you go. As you travel you will pick up more of the language and the more you know, the more you will benefit from your stay. Regional accents and usages vary, but the basic language is essentially the same everywhere.

Vowels

a	as in English *cat*
e	as in English *best*
i	as the ee in English *feet*
o	as in English *shop*
u	as the oo in English *food*
ai	as the i in English *ride*
ei	as ey in English *they*
oi	as oy in English *toy*

Consonants

Most consonants can be pronounced more or less as they are in English. The exceptions are:

g	before *e* or *i* is the same as *j*
h	is always silent (except in *ch* as in *chair*)
j	as the *ch* in Scottish *loch*
ll	as the *y* in *yellow*
ñ	as the *ni* in English *onion*
rr	trilled much more than in English
x	depending on its location, pronounced *x*, *s*, *sh* or *j*

Spanish words and phrases

Greetings, courtesies

hello	*hola*	thank you (very much)	*(muchas) gracias*
good morning	*buenos días*		
good afternoon/evening	*buenas tardes/ noches*	I speak a little Spanish	*hablo un poco de español*
goodbye	*adiós/ hasta luego*	I don't speak Spanish	*no hablo español*
		do you speak English?	*¿hablas inglés?*
pleased to meet you	*encantado/a*	I don't understand	*no entiendo*
how are you?	*¿cómo estás?*	please speak slowly	*habla despacio por favor*
I'm called ...	*me llamo ...*		
what is your name?	*¿cómo te llamas?*	I am very sorry	*lo siento mucho/ discúlpame*
I'm fine, thanks	*muy bien, gracias*	what do you want?	*¿qué quieres?*
		I want/would like	*quiero/quería*
yes/no	*sí/no*	I don't want it	*no lo quiero*
please	*por favor*	good/bad	*bueno/malo*

Basic questions and requests

have you got a room for two people?
  ¿tienes una habitación para dos personas?
how do I get to_?   *¿cómo llego a_?*
how much does it cost?
  ¿cuánto cuesta? ¿cuánto es?
is VAT included?   *¿el IVA está incluido?*
when does the bus leave (arrive)?
  ¿a qué hora sale (llega) el autobús?

when?   *¿cuándo?*
where is_?   *¿dónde está_?*
where can I buy?   *¿dónde puedo comprar...?*
where is the nearest petrol station?
  ¿dónde está la gasolinera más cercana?
why?   *¿por qué?*

Basic words and phrases

bank	*el banco*	market	*el mercado*
bathroom/toilet	*el baño*	note/coin	*el billete/la moneda*
to be	*ser, estar*	police (policeman)	*la policía (el policía)*
bill	*la factura/la cuenta*	post office	*el correo*
cash	*efectivo*	public telephone	*el teléfono público*
cheap	*barato/a*	shop	*la tienda*
credit card	*la tarjeta de crédito*	supermarket	*el supermercado*
exchange rate	*el tipo de cambio*	there is/are	*hay*
expensive	*caro/a*	there isn't/aren't	*no hay*
to go	*ir*	ticket office	*la taquilla*
to have	*tener, haber*	traveller's cheques	*los cheques de viaje*

Getting around

aeroplane	*el avión*	luggage	*el equipaje*
airport	*el aeropuerto*	motorway, freeway	*el autopista/autovía*
arrival/departure	*la llegada/salida*	north/south/ west/east	*el norte, el sur, el oeste, el este*
avenue	*la avenida*	oil	*el aceite*
border	*la frontera*	to park	*aparcar*
bus station	*la estación de autobuses*	passport	*el pasaporte*
		petrol/gasoline	*la gasolina*
bus	*el bus/el autobús/ el camión*	puncture	*el pinchazo*
corner	*la esquina*	street	*la calle*
customs	*la aduana*	that way	*por allí*
left/right	*izquierda/derecha*	this way	*por aquí*
ticket	*el billete*	tyre	*el neumático*
empty/full	*vacío/lleno*	unleaded	*sin plomo*
highway, main road	*la carretera*	waiting room	*la sala de espera*
insurance	*el seguro*	to walk	*caminar/andar*
insured person	*el asegurado/la asegurada*		

Accommodation

air conditioning	*el aire acondicionado*	restaurant	*el restaurante*
all-inclusive	*todo incluido*	room/bedroom	*la habitación*
bathroom, private	*el baño privado*	sheets	*las sábanas*
bed, double	*la cama matrimonial*	shower	*la ducha*
blankets	*las mantas*	soap	*el jabón*
to clean	*limpiar*	toilet	*el inódoro*
dining room	*el comedor*	toilet paper	*el papel higiénico*
hotel	*el hotel*	towels, clean/dirty	*las toallas limpias sucias*
noisy	*ruidoso*	water, hot/cold	*el agua caliente/ fría*
pillows	*las almohadas*		

Health

aspirin	*la aspirina*	diarrhoea	*la diarrea*
blood	*la sangre*	doctor	*el médico*
chemist	*la farmacia*	fever/sweat	*la fiebre/el sudor*
condoms	*los preservativos, los condones*	pain	*el dolor*
contact lenses	*los lentes de contacto*	head	*la cabeza*
		period	*la regla*
contraceptives	*los anticonceptivos*	sanitary towels	*las toallas femeninas*
contraceptive pill	*la píldora anticonceptiva*	stomach	*el estómago*

Family

family	*la familia*	boyfriend/girlfriend	*el novio/la novia*
brother/sister	*el hermano/ la hermana*	friend	*el amigo/ la amiga*
daughter/son	*la hija/el hijo*	married	*casado/a*
father/mother	*el padre/la madre*	single/unmarried	*soltero/a*
husband/wife	*el esposo (marido)/la mujer*		

Months, days and time

January	*enero*	July	*julio*
February	*febrero*	August	*agosto*
March	*marzo*	September	*septiembre*
April	*abril*	October	*octubre*
May	*mayo*	November	*noviembre*
June	*junio*	December	*diciembre*

Monday	*lunes*	it's one o'clock	*es la una*
Tuesday	*martes*	it's seven o'clock	*son las siete*
Wednesday	*miércoles*	it's six twenty	*son las seis y*
Thursday	*jueves*		*veinte*
Friday	*viernes*	it's five to nine	*son las nueve*
Saturday	*sábado*		*menos cinco*
Sunday	*domingo*	in ten minutes	*en diez minutos*
at one o'clock	*a la una*	five hours	*cinco horas*
at half past two	*a las dos y media*	does it take long?	*¿tarda mucho?*
at a quarter to three	*a las tres menos*		
	cuarto		

Numbers

one	*uno*	sixteen	*dieciséis*
two	*dos*	seventeen	*diecisiete*
three	*tres*	eighteen	*dieciocho*
four	*cuatro*	nineteen	*diecinueve*
five	*cinco*	twenty	*veinte*
six	*seis*	twenty-one	*veintiuno*
seven	*siete*	thirty	*treinta*
eight	*ocho*	forty	*cuarenta*
nine	*nueve*	fifty	*cincuenta*
ten	*diez*	sixty	*sesenta*
eleven	*once*	seventy	*setenta*
twelve	*doce*	eighty	*ochenta*
thirteen	*trece*	ninety	*noventa*
fourteen	*catorce*	hundred	*cien/ciento*
fifteen	*quince*	thousand	*mil*

Food glossary

A

acedía	small wedge sole
aceite	oil; *aceite de oliva* is olive oil and *aceite de girasol* is sunflower oil
aceitunas	olives, also sometimes called *olivas*. The best kind are unripe green *manzanilla*, particularly when stuffed with anchovy, *rellenas con anchoas*
adobo	marinated fried nuggets usually of shark (*tiburón*) or dogfish (*cazón*); delicious
agua	water
aguacate	avocado
ahumado	smoked; *tabla de ahumados* is a mixed plate of smoked fish
ajillo (al)	cooked in garlic, most commonly *gambas* or *pollo*
ajo	garlic, *ajetes* are young garlic shoots, often in a *revuelto*
ajo arriero	a simple sauce of garlic, paprika and parsley
ajo blanco	a chilled garlic and almond soup, a speciality of Málaga
albóndigas	meatballs
alcachofa/ alcaucil	artichoke
alcaparras	capers
aliño	any salad marinated in vinegar, olive oil and salt; often made with egg or potato, with chopped onion, peppers and tomato
alioli	a tasty sauce made from raw garlic blended with oil and egg yolk; also called *ajoaceite*
almejas	name applied to various species of small clams, often cooked with garlic, parsley and white wine
almendra	almond
alubias	broad beans
anchoa	preserved anchovy
anchoba/ anjova	bluefish
añejo	aged (of cheeses, rums, etc)
angulas	baby eels, a delicacy that has become scarce and expensive. Far more common are *gulas*, false *angulas* made from putting processed fish through a spaghetti machine; squid ink is used for authentic colouring
anís	aniseed, commonly used to flavour biscuits and liqueurs
arroz	rice; *arroz con leche* is a sweet rice pudding
asado	roast. An *asador* is a restaurant specializing in charcoal-roasted meat and fish
atún	blue-fin tuna
azúcar	sugar

B

bacalao	salted cod, either superb or leathery
berberechos	cockles
berenjena	aubergine/eggplant
besugo	red bream
bistec	steak. *Poco hecho* is rare, *al punto* is medium rare, *regular* is medium, *muy hecho* is well done
bizcocho	sponge cake or biscuit
bocadillo/ bocata	a crusty filled roll
bogavante	lobster
bonito	atlantic bonito, a small tuna fish
boquerones	fresh anchovies, often served filleted in garlic and oil
botella	bottle
(a la) brasa	cooked on a griddle over coals
buey	ox

C

caballa	mackerel
cacahuetes	peanuts
café	coffee; *solo* is black, served espresso-style; *cortado* adds a dash of milk, *con leche* more; *americano* is a long black coffee
calamares	squid
caldereta	a stew of meat or fish usually made with sherry; *venao* (venison) is commonly used, and delicious
caldo	a thin soup
callos	tripe
caña	a glass of draught beer
cangrejo	crab; occasionally river crayfish
caracol	snail; very popular in Sevilla *cabrillas, burgaos,* and *blanquillos* are popular varieties
caramelos	boiled sweets
carne	meat
carta	menu
casero	home-made
castañas	chestnuts
cava	sparkling wine, mostly produced in Catalunya
cazuela	a stew, often of fish or seafood
cebolla	onion
cena	dinner
centollo	spider crab
cerdo	pork
cerezas	cherries
cerveza	beer
champiñón	mushroom
chipirones	small squid, often served *en su tinta,* in its own ink, mixed with butter and garlic
chocolate	a popular afternoon drink; also slang for hashish
choco	cuttlefish
chorizo	a red sausage, versatile and of varying spiciness (*picante*)
choto	roast kid
chuleta/ chuletilla	chop
chuletón	a massive T-bone steak, often sold by weight
churrasco	barbecued meat, often ribs with a spicy sauce
churro	a fried dough-stick usually eaten with hot chocolate (*chocolate con churros*). Usually eaten as a late afternoon snack (*merienda*), but sometimes for breakfast

cigala	Dublin Bay prawn/ Norway lobster
ciruela	plum
cochinillo	suckling pig
cocido	a heavy stew, usually of meat and chickpeas/beans; *sopa de cocido* is the broth
codorniz	quail
cogollo	lettuce heart
comida	lunch
conejo	rabbit
congrio	conger eel
cordero	lamb
costillas	ribs
crema catalana	a lemony crème brûlée
criadillas	hog or bull testicles
croquetas	deep-fried crumbed balls of meat, béchamel, seafood, or vegetables
cuchara	spoon
cuchillo	knife
cuenta (la)	the bill

D

desayuno	breakfast
dorada	a species of bream (gilthead)
dulce	sweet

E

ecológico	organic
embutido	any salami-type sausage
empanada	a pie, pasty-like (*empanadilla*) or in large flat tins and sold by the slice; *atun* or *bonito* is a common filling, as is ham, mince or seafood
ensalada	salad; *mixta* is usually a large serve of a bit of everything; excellent option
ensaladilla rusa	Russian salad, with potato, peas and carrots in mayonnaise
escabeche	pickled in wine and vinegar
espárragos	asparagus, white and usually canned
espinacas	spinach
estofado	braised, often in stew form

F

fabada	the most famous of Asturian dishes, a hearty stew of beans, *chorizo*, and *morcilla*
fideuá	a bit like a paella but with noodles
filete	steak
fino	the classic dry sherry
flamenquín	a fried and crumbed finger of meat stuffed with ham
flan	the ubiquitous crème caramel, great when home-made (*casero*), awful when it's not
foie	fattened goose liver; often made into a thick gravy sauce
frambuesas	raspberries
fresas	strawberries
frito/a	fried
fruta	fruit

G

galletas	biscuits
gallo	rooster, also the flatfish megrim
gambas	prawns
garbanzos	chickpeas, often served in *espinacas con garbanzos*, a spicy spinach dish that is a signature of Seville
gazpacho	a cold garlicky tomato soup, very refreshing

granizado	popular summer drink, like a frappé fruit milkshake	lechuga	lettuce
		lengua	tongue
		lenguado	sole
guisado/ guiso	stewed/a stew	lentejas	lentils
		limón	lemon
guisantes	peas	lomo	loin, usually sliced pork, sometimes tuna
		lubina	sea bass

H

habas	broad beans, often deliciously stewed *con jamón*, with ham
harina	flour
helado	ice cream
hígado	liver
higo	fig
hojaldre	puff pastry
horno (al)	oven (baked)
hueva	fish roe
huevo	egg

I/J

ibérico	see *jamón*; the term can also refer to other pork products
infusión	herbal tea
jabalí	wild boar
jamón	ham; *jamón York* is cooked British-style ham. Far better is cured *jamón serrano*; *ibérico* ham comes from Iberian pigs in western Spain fed on acorns (*bellotas*). Some places, like Jabugo, are famous for their hams, which can be expensive
judías verdes	green beans
jerez (al)	cooked in sherry

L

langosta	crayfish
langostinos	king prawns
lechazo	milk-fed lamb
leche	milk

M

macedonia de frutas	fruit salad, usually tinned
manchego	Spain's national cheese; hard, whitish and made from ewe's milk
manitas (de cerdo)	pork trotters
mantequilla	butter
manzana	apple
manzanilla	the dry, salty sherry from Sanlúcar de Barrameda; also, confusingly, camomile tea and the tastiest type of olive
marisco	shellfish
mejillones	mussels
melocotón	peach, usually canned and served in *almíbar* (syrup)
melva	frigate mackerel, often served tinned or semi-dried
menestra	a vegetable stew, usually served like a minestrone without the liquid; vegetarians will be annoyed to find that it's often seeded with ham and bits of pork
menú	a set meal, usually consisting of three or more courses, bread and wine or water

menudo	tripe stew, usually with chickpeas and mint	parrilla	grill; a *parrillada* is a mixed grill
merluza	hake is to Spain as rice is to southeast Asia	pastel	cake/pastry
mero	grouper	patatas	potatoes; often chips (*patatas fritas*, which confusingly can also refer to crisps); *bravas* are with a spicy tomato sauce
miel	honey		
migas	breadcrumbs, fried and often mixed with lard and meat to form a delicious rural dish of the same name		
		pato	duck
Mojama	salt-cured tuna, most common in Cádiz province	pavía	a crumbed and fried nugget of fish, usually *bacalao* or *merluza*
mollejas	sweetbreads; ie the pancreas of a calf or lamb	pavo	turkey
		pechuga	breast (usually chicken)
montadito	a small toasted filled roll	perdiz	partridge
morcilla	blood sausage, either solid or semi-liquid	pescado	fish
		pescaíto frito	Andalucían deep-fried fish and seafood
morro	cheek, pork or lamb		
mostaza	mustard	pestiños	an Arabic-style confection of pastry and honey, traditionally eaten during Semana Santa
mosto	grape juice. Can also refer to a young wine, from 3 months old		
		pez espada	swordfish; delicious; sometimes called *emperador*

N

naranja	orange		
nata	sweet whipped cream	picadillo	a dish of spicy mincemeat
natillas	rich custard dessert	picante	hot, ie spicy
navajas	razor shells	pichón	squab
nécora	small sea crab, sometimes called a velvet crab	pijota	whiting
		pimienta	pepper
nueces	walnuts	pimientos	peppers; there are many kinds, *piquillos* are the trademark thin Basque red pepper; Padrón produces sweet green mini ones. A popular tapa is *pimientos aliñados* (marinated roasted peppers, often with onion, sometimes with tuna)

O

orejas	ears, usually of a pig
oruro	a fiery grape spirit, often brought to add to black coffee if the waiter likes you
ostras	oysters, also a common expression of dismay

P

paella	rice dish with saffron, seafood and/or meat
pan	bread

pincho	a small snack or grilled meat on a skewer (or *pinchito*)
pipas	sunflower seeds, a common snack
pisto	a ratatouille-like vegetable concoction
plancha (a la)	grilled on a hot iron or fried in a pan without oil
plátano	banana
pluma	a cut of pork next to the loin
pollo	chicken
postre	dessert
potaje	a soup or stew
pringá	a tasty paste of stewed meats usually eaten in a *montadito* and a traditional final tapa of the evening
puerros	leeks
pulpo	octopus, particularly delicious *a la gallega*, boiled Galician style and garnished with olive oil, salt and paprika
puntillitas	small squid, often served crumbed and deep fried

Q/R

queso	cheese; *de cabra* (goat's), *oveja* (sheep's) or *vaca* (cow's). It comes fresh (*fresco*), medium (*semi-curado*) or strong (*curado*)
rabo de buey/toro	oxtail
ración	a portion of food served in cafés and bars; check the size and order a half (*media*) if you want less
rana	frog; *ancas de rana* is frogs' legs
rape	monkfish/anglerfish

raya	any of a variety of rays and skates
rebujito	a weak mix of *manzanilla* and lemonade, consumed by the bucketload during Andalucían festivals
relleno/a	stuffed
reserva, gran reserva, crianza	terms relating to the age of wines; *gran reserva* is the oldest and finest, then *reserva* followed by *crianza*
revuelto	scrambled eggs, usually with wild mushrooms (*setas*) or seafood; often a speciality
riñones	kidneys
rodaballo	turbot; pricey and delicious
romana (à la)	fried in batter
rosca	a large round dish, a cross between sandwich and pizza
rosquilla	doughnut

S

sal	salt
salchicha	sausage
salchichón	a salami-like sausage
salmón	salmon
salmonete	red mullet
salmorejo	a delicious thicker version of gazpacho, often garnished with egg and cured ham
salpicón	a seafood salad with plenty of onion and vinegar
salsa	sauce
San Jacobo	a steak cooked with ham and cheese
sandía	watermelon
sardinas	sardines, delicious grilled

sargo	white sea bream	tomate	tomato
seco	dry	torrijas	a Semana Santa dessert, bread fried in milk and covered in honey and cinnamon
secreto	a cut of pork loin		
sepia	cuttlefish		
serrano	see *jamón*		
setas	wild mushrooms, often superb	tortilla	a Spanish omelette, with potato, egg, olive oil and optional onion; *tortilla francesa* is a French omelette
sidra	cider		
solomillo	beef or pork steak cut from the sirloin bone, deliciously fried in whisky and garlic in Sevilla (*solomillo al whisky*)		
		tostada	toasted, also a toasted breakfast roll eaten with olive oil, tomato or pâté
sopa	soup; *sopa castellana* is a broth with a fried egg, noodles, and bits of ham		
		trucha	trout

U/V

uva	grape
vaso	glass
venado/ venao	venison
verduras	vegetables
vieiras	scallops, also called *veneras*
vino	wine; *blanco* is white, *rosado* or *clarete* is rosé, *tinto* is red

T

tapa	a saucer-sized portion of bar food
tarta	tart or cake
té	tea
tenedor	fork
ternera	veal or young beef
tinto	red wine is *vino tinto*; a *tinto de verano* is mixed with lemonade and ice, a refreshing option
tocino	pork lard; *tocinillo de cielo* is a caramelized egg dessert

Z

zanahoria	carrot
zumo	fruit juice, usually bottled and pricey

Glossary of architectural terms

A

alcázar a Moorish fort

ambulatory a gallery round the chancel and behind the altar

apse vaulted square or rounded recess at the back of a church

archivolt decorative carving around the outer surface of an arch

art deco a style that evolved between the World Wars, based on geometric forms

artesonado ceiling ceiling of carved wooden panels with Islamic motifs popular throughout Spain in the 15th and 16th centuries

ayuntamiento a town hall

azulejo an ornamental ceramic tile

B

Baldacchino an ornate carved canopy above an altar or tomb

Baroque ornate architectural style of the 17th and 18th centuries

bodega a cellar where wine is kept or made; the term also refers to modern wineries and wine shops

buttress a pillar built into a wall to reinforce areas of greatest stress. A flying buttress is set away from the wall; a feature of Gothic architecture

C

capilla a chapel within a church or cathedral

capital the top of column, joining it to another section. Often highly decorated

castillo a castle or fort

catedral a cathedral, ie the seat of a bishop

chancel the area of a church which contains the main altar, usually at the eastern end

chapterhouse area reserved for Bible study in monastery or church

Churrigueresque a particularly ornate form of Spanish Baroque, named after the Churriguera brothers

colegiata a collegiate church, ie one ruled by a chapter of canons

conjunto histórico a tourist-board term referring to an area of historic buildings

convento	a monastery or convent
coro	the area enclosing the choirstalls, often central and completely closed off in Spanish churches
crossing	the centre of a church, where the 'arms' of the cross join

E

ermita	a hermitage or rural chapel

G

Gothic	13th-15th-century style formerly known as pointed style; distinguished externally by pinnacles and tracery around windows, Gothic architecture lays stress on the presence of light

H

hospital	in pilgrimage terms, a place where pilgrims used to be able to rest, receive nourishment and receive medical attention

I

iglesia	a church

L

lobed arch	Moorish arch with depressions in the shape of simple arches
lonja	a guildhall or fish market

M

mocárabes	small concave spaces used as a decorative feature on Moorish ceilings and archways
modernista	a particularly imaginative variant of art nouveau that came out of Catalonia; exemplified by Gaudí
monasterio	a large monastery usually located in a rural area
monstrance	a ceremonial container for displaying the host
Mozarabic	the style of Christian artisans living under Moorish rule
mudéjar	the work of Muslims living under Christian rule after the Reconquest, characterized by ornate brickwork
multifoil	a type of Muslim-influenced arch with consecutive circular depressions
muralla	a city wall

N

nave	the main body of the church, a single or multiple passageway leading (usually) from the western end up to the crossing or high altar
neoclassical	a reaction against the excesses of Spanish Baroque, this 18th- and 19th-century style saw clean lines and symmetry valued above all things

P

palacio   a palace or large residence

patio   an interior courtyard

pediment   triangular section between top of collums and gables

pilaster   pillar attached to the wall

Plateresque   derived from *platero* (silversmith); used to describe a Spanish Renaissance style characterized by finely carved decoration

R

reliquary   a container to hold bones or remains of saints and other holy things

Renaissance   Spanish Renaissance architecture began when classical motifs were used in combination with Gothic elements in the 16th century

retablo   altarpiece or retable formed by many panels often rising to roof level; can be painted or sculptured

Romanesque (románico)   style spread from France in the 11th and 12th centuries, characterized by barrel vaulting, rounded apses and semicircular arches

Romano   Roman

S

sacristy (sacristía)   part of church reserved for priests to prepare for services

soportales   wooden or stone supports for the 1st floor of civic buildings, forming an arcade underneath

stucco (yesería)   moulding mix consisting mainly of plaster; fundamental part of Moorish architecture

Index → Entries in bold refer to maps

FOOTPRINT
Features

Credits

Footprint credits
Editor: Jo Williams
Production and layout: Emma Bryers
Maps: Kevin Feeney
Colour section: Angus Dawson

Publisher: Patrick Dawson
Managing Editor: Felicity Laughton
Administration: Elizabeth Taylor
Advertising sales and marketing:
John Sadler, Kirsty Holmes

Photography credits
Front cover: Mosaic at the Alhambra
Copyright: Toniflap/Dreamstime.com
Back cover top: The Alhambra
Copyright: Marques/Shutterstock
Back cover bottom: Spice stall
Copyright: Andrea Tessadori/
Dreamstime.com

Colour section
Inside front cover: superstock: age
fotostock/age fotostock, Egon Bömsch/
imagebrok/imageBROKER.
Page 1: shutterstock: Karol Kozlowski.
Page 2: superstock: age fotostock/age
fotostock. **Page 4**: shutterstock: Bill Perry,
Massimiliano Pieraccini; superstock:
age fotostock/age fotostock. **Page 5**:
shutterstock: StevanZZ; superstock: Hans
Zaglitsch/imageb/imageBROKER, Hemis.fr/
Hemis.fr. **Page 6**: superstock: Alan Dawson/
age fotostock, age fotostock/age fotostock.
Page 7: shutterstock: Neftali, liquid studios.
Page 8: superstock: age fotostock/
age fotostock.

Printed in Spain by GraphyCems

The content of *Granada 2nd edition* has
been taken directly from Footprint's
Andalucía Handbook 8th edition.

Publishing information
Footprint Granada
2nd edition
© Footprint Handbooks Ltd
April 2015

ISBN: 978 1 910120 24 8
CIP DATA: A catalogue record for this
book is available from the British Library

® Footprint Handbooks and the
Footprint mark are a registered
trademark of Footprint Handbooks Ltd

Published by Footprint
6 Riverside Court
Lower Bristol Road
Bath BA2 3DZ, UK
T +44 (0)1225 469141
F +44 (0)1225 469461
footprinttravelguides.com

Distributed in the USA by
National Book Network, Inc.

Every effort has been made to ensure
that the facts in this guidebook are
accurate. However, travellers should still
obtain advice from consulates, airlines,
etc about travel and visa requirements
before travelling. The authors and
publishers cannot accept responsibility
for any loss, injury or inconvenience
however caused.

All rights reserved. No part of this
publication may be reproduced, stored
in a retrieval system, or transmitted, in
any form or by any means, electronic,
mechanical, photocopying, recording,
or otherwise without the prior
permission of Footprint Handbooks Ltd.